FORECLOSURE A BRAND-NEW ANSWER!

THE EXTRAORDINARY FORECLOSURE TRANSACTION

FEATURES INCLUDE

A Property Owner's Financial Solution

A Secured Investor Aspiration Achieved

A Lender's Complete Financial Fresh Start

MANY WINNERS

The Owner Can Now:
Rescue And Invest 100% Of The Property Equity.

The Lender Can Now:
Immediately Erase A Bad Loan Off The Books And Reinvest Funds.

The Real Estate Broker Can Now:
Achieve A "Foreclosure Free" Exclusive Listing To Sell.

The Bankruptcy Court Can Now:
Solve A Real Estate Bankruptcy With A Money Answer.

WHAT IS NEW

THE EXTRAORDINARY FORECLOSURE TRANSACTION

DISCLAIMER

No part of this book can be transmitted or reproduced in any form, including print, electronic, photocopying, scanning, mechanical, or recording, without prior written permission from the author.

While the author has made utmost efforts to ensure the accuracy of the written content, all readers are advised to follow the information mentioned herein at their own risk. The author cannot be held responsible for any personal or commercial damage caused by the misinterpretation of information. All readers are encouraged to seek professional advice when needed.

This book has been written for information purposes only. Every effort has been made to make this book as complete and accurate as possible. However, there may be mistakes in typography or content. Also, this book provides information only up to the publishing date. Therefore, this book should be used as a guide - not as the ultimate source.

The purpose of this book is to educate. The author and the publisher do not warrant that the information contained in this book is fully complete and shall not be responsible for any errors or omissions. The author and publisher shall have neither liability nor responsibility to any person or entity with respect to any loss or damage caused or alleged to be caused directly or indirectly by this book.

NAMES AND ACRONYMS

Limited Partnership (LP)

Extraordinary Foreclosure Transaction (EFT).
The name of the transaction in the LP.

Foreclosure Answer Affirmed, Inc. (FAA).
Name of the legal entity used to complete the LP/EFT.

Cash investor (CI).
Secured cash investor in the LP.

The name of the foreclosure property owner limited partner in the LP.
The property owner in foreclosure is called simply "Owner"

The agreement between the general partner and limited partners.
Articles of Limited Partnership © (AOP).

The legal notification of a foreclosure starting.
Notice of Default (NOD).

The name of the funds invested by the CI in the LP.
Critical cash capital (CCC).

The capital accumulation fund in a limited LP.
Operating & investment fund (Q&IF)

TABLE OF CONTENTS

HELPING INSTEAD OF TAKING

The word foreclosure for many people automatically has a negative connotation. However, in the case of the EFT within the LP, any negative assumption one might make because of its involvement with foreclosure does not apply. The foundation of this fresh approach is a very positive attitude towards helping the property owner in foreclosure. Property Owners, Real Estate Brokers, Lenders, Bankruptcy Courts and the LP CI will all benefit with this "foreclosure financial answer".

A unique legal, financial, and investment prototype in a LP has been designed especially to rescue property equities from foreclosure for property owners. The Extraordinary Foreclosure Transaction (EFT) in the LP is an abstract configuration of an idea, reduced to writing, which initiates an innovative legal pattern of operation that forms and produces an answer to a major foreclosure "financial problem" that has never been accomplished before!

The LP/EFT is a three-party real estate transaction between a property owner in foreclosure, a secured Cash Investor (CI), and the Limited Partnership (LP). The LP features two types of very different cash investors in the same LP, a CI and a property owner in foreclosure, that is turned into a cash investor. The foreclosure owner contributes property to the LP that will act as collateral to secure the CI, once the property is taken out of foreclosure. Each type of limited partner, the CI and the property owner turned into an investor by the LP, have individual type investments and different legal standings in the LP.

A REAL BONA FIDE ANSWER

The LP/EFT has been originated to and does rescue property equities from foreclosure, for the full and complete financial benefit of the property owners. There is no other way in the general marketplace for the owner to rescue one hundred (100%) of a substantial equity in a property from being foreclosed. The LP/EFT for the first time ever, initiates an innovative pattern of legal and financial arrangements that form and produces a unique answer to a major foreclosure "financial problem" never accomplished before!

The LP/EFT investment configuration affords a property owner in foreclosure and a qualified CI a unique way to safely invest together as limited partners. It offers a positive solution that will rescue all the property equity from a pending foreclosure and offers a fresh financial start for the owners by turning the currently financial insolvent owners into qualified investors.

The investment capital gathered from rescuing property equities by the LP is invested for the benefit of the property owners rescued from foreclosure. The LP pays a profit share and grows the owner's rescued equity amount. The LP/EFT offers the owner the most attractive foreclosure equity loss solution available anywhere!

Never in the foreclosure market has there been developed an answer wherein the owner of the property being foreclosed upon could obtain a full value price for the property. Now the owner has a real choice of selling their property for full value and investing the rescued money by choosing the LP/EFT. This one-of-a-kind opportunity is the only positive choice for an owner who cannot solve the problem. By joining the LP as a limited partner, the owner attracts the necessary money and time with which to restructure his or her present financial status.

The owner by choosing to become a qualified investor in an LP/EFT can make their capital grow and avoid all the negative consequences of foreclosure. For those who find they have run out of solutions and time to avoid a giveaway sale or forced sale at auction, the LP/EFT offers the only viable alternative.

A REMARKABLE ANSWER DESIGNED

Foreclosure in the United States is a major problem for many thousands of property owners every year. In this book a description of the property owner's foreclosure situation is put forward, along with a comprehensive answer, that expresses and embodies a favorable answer for the owners. A solution that will provide a much-needed fair and just answer to those in foreclosure. The need for a foreclosure solution is great and the LP/EFT is the only bona fide answer.

An original foreclosure money answer for property owners in need has been created. The owner under severe financial duress is helped to become a qualified investor in a new exclusive arrangement. The owner's entire equity (100%) in the property is rescued and grows with profit share while all the present and future ugly consequences of a foreclosure are avoided for the owners. This answer is not found in any other investment and is truly a unique development that saves a financial catastrophe from occurring to the property owner.

The LP/EFT answer provides a property owner with the rescue of all their property equity from loss due to foreclosure. Also, it allows the rescued owner's equity to substantially grow with a profit share as a limited partner investor in the LP. At the same time the answer eliminates entirely all the painful negative financial and legal consequences a foreclosure would cause the owner. There is no charge to the owner for the service and use of the intellectual plan provided to rescue the equity.

No other real answer then the LP/EFT is offered or possible! Many answers to solve a foreclosure are claimed by individuals. Some are "negotiate with the lender", make a "short sale", or give "a deed in lieu of foreclosure". Of course, none of these so called "answers" create any money with which the owners can even begin to "solve" the foreclosure and save their credit and property equity. Instead, they are "stalling" or "give up techniques" and, in the final analysis, do not help the property owners in foreclosure. The truth is only one thing will solve a foreclosure. Money is the only thing that will solve the problem, and the money is arranged to cure the foreclosure and sell the property for full value for the property owner in the LP/EFT!

Foreclosure is not only the owner's problem, but it is also a societal problem. The process is unfair because the financial punishment is so very severe. Loss of years of supporting the monthly property payments to build-up the equity as a nest egg for retirement is lost. Most important also is that the nasty aftereffects of a foreclosure have serious and long-term legal and financial consequences. All current and long-term negative financial and legal consequences a foreclosure cause is eliminated in the LP/EFT for the owners.

TIME AND TIME AGAIN

Each year hundreds of thousands of property owners throughout the United States lose their financial nest egg that was planned for retirement through foreclosure. Here is the standard everyday foreclosure problem, a property owner goes into foreclosure with a substantial amount of equity in the property and no way to pay the Notice of Default arrearage that started the foreclosure proceeding. The owner is then subject to a giveaway sale for pennies on the dollar or to losing the equity in a forced foreclosure auction.

The technical meaning of the word foreclosure is to wipe out a right of redemption on a property. Generally, this is what happens when someone does not pay his or her mortgage. Even though there have been no payments, the borrower retains an equitable right of redemption if, some day, he or she were able to find the money and try to exercise their right of redemption. To clear the title of this potential, a lender goes to court, demonstrates the default, requests that a date be set where the entire amount becomes payable after which, in the absence of payment, the lender is automatically relieved of the requirement to redeem the property back to the borrower; the debtor's right of redemption is said to be forever barred and foreclosed. This cancels all rights a borrower would have in the property and the property then belongs entirely to the lender, who is then free to possess or sell the property. The word is frequently used to generally refer to the lender's actions of repossessing and selling a property for default in mortgage payments.

The foreclosure process of closing out property ownership and causing the owner to lose the property equity will continue forever. There is no other way to protect the money loaned on the property by the lender when an owner cannot pay as agreed. There are hundreds of thousands of default notices that start the foreclosure process sent to property owners each year in the United States. There has never been a positive financial solution for property owners throughout the United States in this circumstance until now.

THE CAUSE OF FORECLOSURE

Money problems cause foreclosure. The financial activity of the general economy influences the number of foreclosures, however some items causing foreclosures have nothing to do with the market conditions and will always go on and on. Financial problems causing foreclosure are divorce, drugs, death, poor money management, medical bills, college costs, accidents, bad business decisions, bad business market trends, employment displacement causing lower income, high-rate interest only loans, and loan payments that are in flux because of adjustable rate. These problems will never go away and will be repeated daily forever involving thousands of owners throughout the United States.

A fact that is unchallengeable in the United States; there are billions and billions of hard-earned dollars lost each year by property owners because of foreclosure. History teaches and confirms this. Foolish to argue with a fact that is indisputable. When it is realized that 43% of American households spend more than they earn each year and 60% or more live from paycheck to paycheck, it is not difficult to understand why so many property owners go into foreclosure each year! Poor distribution of limited earnings cause foreclosure!

Anyone can see that when lenders grant a loan, they have no way of telling what negative influences might happen to a very qualified borrower as time goes on. Millions of loans are granted by lenders every year. Therefore, there will always be, without question, a very large number of foreclosures occurring each year in the United States.

There are a lot of foreclosures started and completed by the lenders that are recorded that can and are counted, and they are substantial in number. In recent history a million of foreclosure properties in a year have been recorded in the United States. In the pipeline (some in bankruptcy) there is always a couple of million properties in the foreclosure on going pipeline. Now there is only one way for the owner to cure a foreclosure and rescue all (100%) the property equity. The LP/EFT rescues and invests all the equity for the owner instead of the owner losing the equity.

A BAD OR GOOD CHOICE

When a property owner faces a foreclosure, it becomes emotionally and financially devastating because their major financial security is at serious risk. The homeowner is financially insolvent now, and the owner's property in foreclosure is highly leveraged to the point where the owner cannot borrow funds to cure the Notice of Default, foreclosure is inevitable, without the LP/EFT.

The only choice current market answers offered the owner, who cannot solve the foreclosure himself or herself, are financial disasters for the owners. The owner can sell the property, under duress of a pending foreclosure at a below market value and take a severe loss, which is not an answer at all. Or the owner will lose the property to a foreclosure trustee sale, another financial disaster for the owner. Going to a "foreclosure trustee sale" is not an acceptable answer for the owners in foreclosure, with this type of finality they lose most or all the equity they have build-up over the years. These are the only two avenues an owner has if the owner does not have or cannot borrow the money to cure the Notice of Default.

When an owner has no money and no credit and is about to lose the property ownership along with its hard-earned equity what is the owner to do? The LP/EFT can now help the owner save all the equity from foreclosure by arranging the funds to cure the foreclosure. For owners with a pending foreclosure with only two choices available, that cannot be compared to the financial benefit the new LP/EFT provides, the choice is clear. The LP/EFT is the answer that will save all the owner's equity.

Foreclosure is a serious problem for the owner that society has been concerned with forever. No fair and acceptable answer to foreclosure for the owner has ever been found until now. Now there is a fair and honest way to solve foreclosure and rescue the equity for the property owners. The LP/EFT provides a real groundbreaking way for owners to receive the financial help needed.

OWNER LACKS CONTRACTUAL UNDERSTANDING

The owner should know, but often does not realize what really happens, if contractual loan terms and conditions are not kept the process of foreclosure will begin! When terms of a loan contract are breached and a Notice of Default is filed, the immediate result for the owner becomes a series of problems such as: money, timing, low sale offers, and professional help difficulties. The problem for the owners first starts out to be a money problem then it becomes both a money and time problem, then it becomes a money-time-low offer problem. If there is no money answer found in time, both the property with all the equity is lost! All these are serious problems for an owner to deal with, to find an answer within a limited time frame.

The owner does not know the foreclosure procedure and the difficulties associated with the process until the owner receives the Notice of Default. It takes time to learn what this information means, and this exasperates the problem by using up the little time allotted to cure the foreclosure. If time goes by without the problem being cured, it gets worse for the property owners. It leaves them vulnerable to a solution that is made unbearable under duress and will cause the loss of all their money.

THE FORECLOSURE OWNER'S TIME LIMIT
The owner has a limited time to cure the default. Under the foreclosure law in most states time to cure is limited to a relatively short time (approximately 3 months) for the owner to find the money necessary to cure the foreclosure. The foreclosure problem starts for the owner when a Notice of Default is filed on the owner's property that has legal regulations designed to take the title from the owner. To cure the default the time limit allowed to cure must be met by the owner or the property and remaining equity will be foreclosed upon and lost.

WHAT REALLY HAPPENS IN THE MARKET PLACE
No person whether a qualified new buyer or a foreclosure profit speculator will pay the full fair market value of the property in the process of being foreclosed. Everyone purchasing property for whatever reason always offers the lowest price to purchase the property. In the case of a property in foreclosure the amount offered to the owner usually **equals the loan balance due plus a few thousand dollars**. That is what really happens because the buyer always looks to buy for the lowest price so profit can be maximized. Yes, this fact has been proven over the years' time and time again! No one walks up to an owner in the foreclosure process and says because you are in dire financial straits I will pay the full market value for your property. A home buyer or profit speculator will take all the owner's equity every time for little or nothing. This happens every day throughout the United States, it is a fact.

There is a "foreclosure profit speculator system" throughout the United States that takes financial advantage of an owner in foreclosure in no uncertain terms. The profit speculator takes advantage of the owner by telling the owner that the owner's credit will be saved by avoiding foreclosure. The profit speculator does nothing else for the property owner. The speculator takes the property ownership by only paying pennies on the dollar and keeps several thousands of dollars of the owner's property equity. It is like being a bank robber without going to prison. Foreclosure profit speculating is not a nice thing to do. However, it is not against the law and the speculator did not cause the owners problem, so they can do it!

In considering how to determine if enough properties go into foreclosure in the United States that makes the LP/EFT viable, one must consider the total number of properties lost to foreclosure speculators each year. I don't think anyone knows how many properties are purchased and taken out of foreclosure by a profit speculator each year in the United States, that are recorded as normal property sales. A good guess would be several hundred thousand properties netting billions of dollars to the speculators!

The property equity took the owners years to accumulate by faithfully making loan payments on time. It is a terrible blow to lose the equity after paying in so much over several years to create a large equity position.

FORECLOSURE HELP VS PROFIT SPECULATION

Foreclosure Speculator Says:

"I can avoid the foreclosure for you and save your credit". The foreclosure profit speculator avoids the foreclosure for the owner at the expense of all the owners' equity. Saving your credit and losing all your equity does not seem like a good idea. Most people would rather have all the equity saved for them to invest when the property is sold at full value by the LP. The LP/EFT rescues all the equity for the owners and the foreclosure is also avoided!

After reviewing and understanding the foreclosure owner's problem you can see why the foreclosure profit speculator is successful in convincing the owners to give up their hard-earned equity. The owner in most cases cannot solve the foreclosure money problem and loses the property most of the time due to timing and duress caused by the foreclosure process.

The hard-earned equity in many cases is very substantial. A fair estimate is that fifty percent (50%) or more of properties in foreclosure have twenty-five percent (25%) of the property value or more as equity. Twenty-five percent (25%) of a property valued at $400,000 has a remaining equity of $100,000 in the property being foreclosed. Now using the LP/EFT, the property foreclosure can be cured, and the property can be sold at full market price for the owners. One hundred percent of the $100,000 equity can now be rescued for the owner's sole benefit.

The speculator gains big by offering a low price to the owner who walks away with little or nothing at all. The speculator pays less than full value for the property and then will sell it for full value. The speculator keeps the cash difference, it is really the owner's money (equity) being taken for nothing in return!

EXAMPLES NOT ACTUAL CASE

AVERAGE $300,000 PROPERTY RESCUE ESTIMATE

$300,000 + Appraised value

$180,000 - 60% LTV

$ 15,000 - NOD Late Payments 5% LTV

_____

$105,000 + Gross Property Equity

$ 18,000 - 6% Selling Commission

$ 12,000 - All Closing Cost

_____

$ 75,000 + Net Equity to Rescue and Invest in the LP.

A MILLION-DOLLAR PROPERTY NOTICE OF DEFAULT ESTIMATE

There is a saying, "the bigger they are the harder they fall". Many high-priced properties receive a Notice of Default is recorded against them each year! How many million-dollar properties are they like this? The answer is an awful lot!

$1,000,000 + Appraised Property Value

$ 650,000 - 65% Loan Principal Balance

$ 50,000 - 05% NOD Late Payments & Foreclosure Costs

$ 60,000 - 06% Sale Commission

$ 30,000 - All Selling and Closing Cost

_____

$ 210,000 + Owner Net Equity to Rescue and Invest in the LP.

NOTE: Depending on the amount and the owner's need, the equity amount that will be invested in the LP can be negotiated. It is not necessary for the owner in some cases to invest the whole equity amount. Reason will prevail, helping the owner is the goal.

How could a profit speculator buying for profit create a different financial way of achieving the same 100% financial result for the owner that the LP/EFT does? The numbers would make it clear; it is not possible for a speculator to offer the same 100% result as the LP/EFT does.

What speculator would put up the capital required to cure the foreclosure costs and take all the legal and financial responsibility of ownership and then share the equity with the owner? This does not make sense and history over centuries verifies that it does not happen! In the case of a property in foreclosure the amount offered to the owner by a speculator usually equals a few thousand dollars. The profit speculator takes all the equity from the owner to maximize profit every time.

THE SCARY FORECLOSURE PENALTIES

As each person's financial well-being is paramount and establishing an earning system that will build wealth is critical. An established way in the United States of America to earn and build a comfortable retirement fund is to own real estate (private residence) that will increase in value over time. Millions of Americans use this method to be financially secure later in life.

However, a foreclosure can cause a complete loss of property equity, if the loan is not paid on time as agreed. A pending foreclosure against property, if completed cause the owner very serious legal and financial consequences such as:
1. A loss of the entire equity remaining in the property.
2. A harsh long-term financial cost and credit damage.
3. A loss of investor status and future earnings.
4. A foreclosure wipes out a junior lender's security and can cause a lawsuit against the owner to collect the money loaned.
5. A capital gain tax because of mortgage over basis after foreclosure, without the equity to pay the tax.
6. A major mental pain caused from losing all the money.

A NEW LP OPERATING & INVESTMENT FUND (O&IF)

The LP Extraordinary Foreclosure Transaction is revolutionary. Not every real estate transaction has so much to offer as the EFT does. By designing the EFT to rescue equities from foreclosure that raises operating and investment capital in large amounts quickly a new method is created.

While helping owners with one of the most serious financial problems they have is most gratifying, the LP/EFT main reason is to earn profit by creating a Q&IF in each LP started. By designing the LP to rescue equities from foreclosure to raise investment capital in large amounts quickly, the LP becomes a leader! Never has such an ability been developed to gather so much investment capital in a Q&IF on a never-ending ever-increasing basis.

The LP can raise millions of dollars of investment capital throughout the United States by helping property owners rescue their property equity from foreclosure. The capital fund will accumulate exponentially, allowing for extremely safe and rewarding investments to be formulated for the first time that involve financial problems.

When several individual LPs are operating each O&IF in a LP can gather investment capital. The LPs will garner investment capital forever because many foreclosures will occur each year in the USA forever. This powerful way to gather large sums of investment capital this way is a first-time achievement.

Financial problems that cannot be addressed without substantial reserve cash to ensure success can now be taken on and answered. A variety of new investment and financial opportunities can be profitable because of the Q&IF. The Q&IF will be a financial source for providing answers to many different real estate money problems, not just foreclosure problems.

In the LP/EFT the property owners are rescued from foreclosure and are converted from a current financially insolvent position, because of a pending foreclosure, into a qualified investor. By the LP/EFT turning the owners into investor partners using the property equities rescued as investment funds it creates an ever-growing never-ending Operating and Investment Fund (Q&IF) to invest for the owner's benefits. The owner's equity amount rescued will grow with a share of profit earned.

THE LP INNOVATIVE O&IF CAN

Because of the O&IF amount will be always growing the LP can create original investment transactions that otherwise could not be designed.

Because of the LP Operating and Investment Fund all kinds of property problems can be entertained with real solutions that will work. Many financial problems with properties are dismissed as unsolvable because of the money necessary to solve the problem. New construction, old repairable problems, improvements required by law for any reason can be entertained by the LP because it has the Operating and Investment Fund to achieve solving the problem.

Because of the size of the average LP O&IF the LP can back up an initial amount of investment funds in an investment and minimize the risk factor. The fact that it will have a serious amount of backup funds to ensure financial needs solidifies the success of the investment.

Because of the O&IF capacity to grow exponentially, the LP can invest in transactions that otherwise could not be attempted, due to a very large financial requirement.

Because of the O&IF many different types of financial opportunities can be created to earn profit that will be shared by the LP partners.

FORECLOSURE ANSWER BENEFITS LENDER

The lenders gain from a financial standpoint, which has a very positive and substantial effect on their business. Currently, lenders are required by federal government to set aside a reserve for each loan in default and this is eating away at the profit margin. Lenders will appreciate the financial improvement by having bad loans cured and then taken off the books. The lenders will have a reduction in federal government bad loan reserve requirement because of fewer bad loans on the books, thanks to the LP/EFT solving foreclosures, and will have more money to lend.

There will always be, without question, a very large number of foreclosures occurring each year throughout the United States. This is because the lenders who loan money do not have a crystal ball. The lender can review a loan application very carefully. However, they will never know what will happen to the borrower that will change his or her financial standing in a negative way as time goes on. This is the reason the lender's judgment is good only for a moment in time. This phenomenon is built into the process and many reversals of the borrower's positive financial status cause foreclosures to occur regularly.

The institutional lenders such as banks and savings and loans generally will not lend into a property that has a Notice of Default (NOD) recorded against it. A general rule is the equity lender will not lend money over seventy-five (75%) loan to value. And the equity lender lending must qualify the borrower to the extent the borrower can pay the monthly debt service, before loaning more money. The owner is already financially overburdened as he/she cannot pay the current monthly loan amount. No lender will lend money unless there is enough equity to cover the loan amount and expensive cost to collect the equity lender's loan granted. Any loan granted from an equity lender must be protected with sufficient equity.

There are thousands of Notices of Defaults that start the foreclosure process sent to property owners each year in the United States by lenders. The century old foreclosure process of closing out ownership and causing the owner to lose all the equity will continue forever as there is no other way to protect the lenders. There has never been a financial honest solution for the thousands of property owners throughout the United States in this circumstance until now.

FORECLOSURE HISTORICAL FACTS SET IN CEMENT

When the following foreclosure facts are understood it comes clear that the need for the LP/EFT will go on forever.

The Lender Lending Rules

The institutional lenders such as banks and savings and loans will not generally loan on a property that has a Notice of Default (NOD) recorded against it. The general rule for equity lenders is that they will not lend money more than 75% loan to value. No lender will lend money unless there is enough equity to cover the loan amount and cost to collect, in case of a default.

This will never change!

The Foreclosure Law

The laws regarding foreclosure are geared to legally recover the collateral (property) in case the loan is defaulted upon. So, if the loan is defaulted upon the lender must foreclose and sell the property to collect the funds loaned.

This will never change!

Foreclosure Market Will Always increase

There will always be several foreclosures increasing, this is because the lenders who loan money do not have a crystal ball. The lender can review a loan application very carefully. However, they do not know what will happen to the borrower that will change his or her financial standing in a negative way as time goes on. This is the reason the lender's judgment is good only for a moment in time. This foreclosure phenomenon is built into the lending process.

This will never change!

Foreclosures Will Increase as The Population Does

The number of foreclosures will always grow because of the number of new properties built that could go into foreclosure in the future. Also, there are a multiple of financial reasons why an owner of property cannot pay the loan payment that cause a default. With these reasons and the new amount of building that continually goes on one can see that there will forever be foreclosure occurring throughout the USA.

This will never change!

Human Nature Causes the Owner Problem

No person whether a qualified new buyer or a foreclosure profit speculator will pay the full fair market value of the property in the process of being foreclosed. Everyone purchasing property for whatever reason always offers the lowest price to purchase a property. In the case of a property in foreclosure in duress the amount offered to the owner usually equals the loan value plus a few thousand dollars.

This will never change!9

THE LP/EFT IS ORIGINAL

When one understands how the LP/EFT works and what it does for the owner in foreclosure one could ask the question. What owner would refuse to participate in the LP/EFT? Who would give up an opportunity to rescue all his or her hard-earned equity and make it grow in lieu of losing the equity. Refusing the offer to participate in the LP/EFT means that the owner would have to submit to a forced sale at a foreclosure auction or for a sale for pennies on the dollar to a profit speculator.

PART TWO
OWNER SECTION

THE NEED IS GREAT

No other "financial relief" except for the LP/EFT is available for hundreds of thousands of property owners with a pending foreclosure that occur each year throughout the United States. Foreclosure happens daily in the United States and has been going on for centuries. There is a long history of billions of dollars lost by the property owners each year. Every owner with property equity to close due to financial constraints caused by foreclosure needs the LP/EFT program answer. By joining the LP/EFT, the owner's total property equity is rescued for the owner at no cost to the owner. Only the LP/EFT exclusively has and can provide honest, fair, and complete answer to the foreclosure problem for property owners.

SAVING THE FINANCIAL FUTURE

Never before the LP/EFT could the owner in a difficult process of foreclosure, that the owner cannot solve, cure the foreclosure and rescue all their money to invest. The purpose of the property owner joining the LP is to save the property equity from foreclosure and invest it to earn future income!

Imagine being a property owner facing imminent foreclosure on a property that has a substantial equity to lose. Time to find the money to cure the foreclosure is running out and the owner is only receiving pennies on the dollar offers. If the property is sold at a "for sale auction", the owner's major investment nest egg will be gone. The LP/EFT prevents this happening to the owner as the Notice of Default is cured and a foreclosure is avoided.

The LP/EFT has people in dire financial straits immediately eliminate the horror of foreclosure and gain control of their financial status. After becoming financially sound by avoiding foreclosure, owners can begin taking steps towards total financial recovery. The LP/EFT offers the owners an attractive foreclosure equity loss solution for the first-time ever! When considering these accomplishments for the owner it becomes clear that the LP/EFT is indeed providing a very big helping hand at a critical time without cost of any kind.

FORECLOSURE FROM PENDING DISASTER TO A NEW START

The property owner with a pending foreclosure is a new type of limited partner "property investor" in the LP/EFT. Even though the owner is in foreclosure financial trouble, it becomes possible for the owner to invest the property while in foreclosure and

14

save all the property equity to invest. The foreclosed owner becomes a qualified investor in a LP and, the property turns into investment capital after the property is rescued from foreclosure and sold by the LP.

This owner conversion to a qualified cash investor is the foundation of a new way to raise investment funds on a never-ending always-increasing basis for the LP. While helping people solve their foreclosure problems can be a very rewarding and gratifying experience, the main purpose of the LP/EFT is to raise investment capital. The LP can earn profit for itself and all the property owners, that were once in foreclosure and have become limited partners as financially qualified investors.

Two special property owner occurrences. A property owners foreclosure situation is a clear and serious problem that now can be solved in favor of the property owner by the LP. First important happening for the owner is the fact that the property foreclosure is cured by the LP. Next the owner becomes a "cash investor" in the LP with the investment of the property sale proceeds, when the property is sold by the LP. The rescued equity grows in amount by earning a share of the investment profits of the LP.

OWNER HAS A SERIOUS SITUATION
When a property has a foreclosure pending the owner becomes vulnerable to the pressure of time, lack of money, and the owner's negative financial standing. Together these problems make the Notice of Default extremely difficult to solve. The owner is in an untenable situation that requires money and timely attention that the owner does not have. The financial duress the owner is under because of a pending foreclosure makes it impossible to sell the real estate for full market value. The LP/EFT is for the owner who does not have or cannot find the money to solve the foreclosure NOD in time.

THE OWNER'S CONDITION
The owners in foreclosure are faced with many serious problems and need to join the LP/EFT or suffer serious financial consequences. The owner needs to solve all the serious problems, the LP/EFT does exactly that for the owner.
The owner has:
- A mortgage payment that is several months behind.
- No personal funds with which to cure the foreclosure.
- No borrowing is possible on highly leveraged property.
- Personal insolvency disqualifies owner from borrowing more.
- Little time to find money to pay loan arrearage and costs.
- A long-term financial problem due to negative credit report.
- A capital gains tax if any is due after foreclosure.

- A tax due without property equity to pay the tax after foreclosure.
- A collection lawsuit for a junior note that was wiped out.
- A lack of ability to negotiate a fair price property sale.
- A lack of any solution in the general marketplace.

THE OWNER NEEDS A GREAT DEAL
The owner needs:
- To have the notice of default cured immediately.
- To find an answer to rescue the equity.
- To find an infusion of cash to cure a foreclosure when the owner is financially insolvent and has no borrowing ability.
- To immediately lower the risk by curing the foreclosure.
- To rescue the equity to restructure financial standing.
- To invest to make the money grow during the financial restructuring period.
- To eliminate an unaffordable monthly payment.
- To retain equity for future purchasing power.
- To change a negative ongoing long-term credit problem.

AVOIDING IS AS IMPORTANT AS SOLVING
Here are ugly financial and legal consequences eliminated by the LP for the owner.
- Avoiding the loss the entire equity in the property.
- Avoiding years of expensive credit damage.
- Avoiding loss of investment leverage.
- Avoiding loss of future earning opportunity.
- Avoiding starting over with no money and no credit.
- Avoiding harsh long-term financing costs, a foreclosure causes.
- Avoiding a junior lender lawsuit for the note foreclosure wiped out.

RECOGNIZING SPECIAL ACTIVITY
The LP/EFT introduces secured investment funds in a different and better way to cure a Notice of Default. The owner could not cure the NOD because the property in foreclosure is highly leveraged, and the property owner personally is currently financially insolvent. Both the property itself and the owner do not qualify to borrow more money needed. This with as much as twenty-five percent (25%) or more of the property's total value remaining. The LP/EFT provides the necessary funds to the owner to solve the foreclosure.
The LP/EFT is particularly designed to:

- Rescue 100% of the property equity for the owner and make it grow, instead of the owner losing the equity because the owner could not cure the default in time.
- Change a potential sale under duress by the owner, which would cause an "under duress sale" give way for pennies on the dollar, because it is in the process of being foreclosed upon, into a sale at "arms-length" that will achieve a full value sale for the owner.
- Immediately change a financially insolvent property owner into a qualified "cash investor" by having the owner use the rescued equity as investment capital, so that the equity can grow in amount and create future purchasing power.
- Grant the secured CI individual legal positions in the LP/ that provides extraordinary legal, financial, and reward protections never offered before in a real estate transaction. This set of CI protections in the LP/EFT coupled with a "Bonus" payment system adds up for the CI to a very safe and rewarding investment!
- Fashion original real estate transactions. The LP shapes and creates ways to operate "standard every day real estate transactions" into an improved financial structure that is safer. There are transactions arranged using the large Operational and Investment Fund (O&IF), that fashion "unique brand-new real estate transactions". This large growing Q&IF can create and solve different investment financial problems and create unique investment scenarios.
- To cure a property owner's foreclosure financial problem. The LP investment configuration affords a property owner in foreclosure and a qualified CI a unique way to "safely invest together" as limited partners to cure the financial problem and invest in the LP.

THE OWNER'S "RESCUE" & "INVEST OPPORTUNITY"

The LP/EFT is groundbreaking in that it features a way to solve the serious foreclosure problem in a legal and fair way for the property owner and lender. The LP/EFT is for the property owner who does not have or cannot find the money to solve the foreclosure Notice of Default (NOD). With a never-before constructed legal and financial method specially designed to achieve helping a property owner, it becomes possible for the property owner with a serious money problem to solve the problem.

With a unique LP/EFT legal, financial, and investment arrangement, the owner avoids the foreclosure and loss of equity and all the negative consequences a foreclosure might cause. Any loan balance, tax, or legal problem a foreclosure would cause is completely extinguished for the owner. The owner immediately eliminates the horror of foreclosure and gains the opportunity to improve their current financial status. LP/EFT offers the owners the most attractive foreclosure equity loss solution available anywhere!

By joining LP/EFT the owner rescues the property equity to invest in the LP. The owner becomes a qualified investor in a LP by investing the property equity rescued, after the property is taken out of foreclosure and sold by the LP. The LP grows the equity rescued thought investing it and with profit share enhances the owner's future purchasing power. The LP rescues the equity for the owner without charge.

THE OWNER WINS

By arranging a set of unique legal, financial and investment advantages for the owner, designed especially to solve the property owner's dire money-time problem, the LP/EFT can help the owners avoid the foreclosure and prevent the loss their equity. It rescues the property equity for the owner and increases the rescued amount by converting the owner from a financially insolvent property owner into a qualified investor earning profit.

The owner in the foreclosure process using the LP/EFT avoids incurring harsh long-term financing costs because of what a concluded foreclosure would cause. Any loan balance, tax or legal problem a foreclosure would cause the owner is eliminated.

Several things happen for the owner:
- Curing of the Notice of Default
- Accomplishing a full value sale of the property
- Rescuing the entire property equity.
- Accomplishing a full value sale in the general market.
- Maintaining an investor status sharing profit as a partner.
- Growing the rescued property equity.
- Generate future purchasing power.
- Having the property principal loan balance paid off.
- Lowering the high-risk position a pending foreclosure cause.
- Gaining time to reorganize to become financially stable.
- Avoiding all the negative financial consequences a foreclosure causes, such as long-term bad credit, potential lawsuits, and a loss of equity.
- Owner does not pay a dime for the plan and expertise of the general partner.

Note: when you consider that these things are avoided for the owner, at no cost to the owner, it becomes clear that the LP/EFT is indeed providing a very big helping hand for the owner. Do you think the owner would choose to lose the money or save and grow the rescued equity using the LP/EFT?

PROVIDING THE HELP

A legal and financial investment prototype in a LP has been designed that will rescue property equities from foreclosure for the complete benefit of the property owners. If a real estate broker were asked, from an owner of property who cannot borrow money to cure an ongoing foreclosure, can you help me to avoid losing all my property equity built-up over years to foreclosure? The professional will have to answer, sorry if you cannot pay the default amount required in time, I know of no way for you to save all your property equity from being lost. Now, the LP changes the professional's answer to "yes I know of a way". Now the rescue of 100% of the equity can be achieved without cost using the EFT.

If you were the owner in the process of foreclosure, looking for a money answer to save the property equity, would you choose to join to avoid foreclosure and rescue the equity? The owner is given a choice to join that would be difficult to decline! The alternative is a giveaway sale or a forced sale at auction and would be devastating in every way for the owner.

THE DIFFICULT FORECLOSURE MONEY PROBLEM

The financial status of a typical property owner in foreclosure. The owner needs to find the money to solve the foreclosure in a very limited time. The property's debt structure is highly leveraged, and the owner is financially insolvent due to a pending foreclosure. Under these circumstances, borrowing more money to cure a foreclosure is very difficult or impossible in many cases. The owner's effort generally fails as their borrowing ability is next to nil while in foreclosure. This situation occurs "hundreds of thousands of times yearly" in the United States. History tells us the high number of foreclosures repeating will continue to happen forever!

Money is the problem! The owner is bewildered without an actual past foreclosure experience that teaches a correct understanding of what is happening. It is difficult for a person to understand the legal and financial foreclosure process that is happening to them first time around. Owners unfamiliar with the foreclosure process think that because the property has twenty percent (20%) or thirty percent (30%) equity that it is still possible to borrow against it to cure the foreclosure. The amount of equity in the property in many cases will not by itself attract new money to cure the foreclosure. Other decision-making factors play heavily in the lenders mind to lend more money.

MONEY PICTURE

Lending more money to the owner may bring the total owing to eighty percent (80%) LTV or higher that creates a much larger monthly payment. The private lenders and financial institutions have state and federal rules and regulations and need security in the form of enough equity to protect themselves. Regular lending institutions such as savings and loans generally will not lend into a Notice of Default recorded against a property. Banks have state and federal rules and regulations to abide by and stockholders that frown on lending more money to a property owner that has a defaulted loan on going. This is a serious problem for the owner, who needs to borrow funds against a property to solve a pending foreclosure.

Generally, if a property has a seventy-five percent (75%) or higher LTV (loan to value), private equity lenders, called "Hard Money Lenders", will not loan more funds against the property. This is because there needs to be a cushion represented in the remaining amount of equity to protect the new loan amount. And the owner must qualify income wise to borrow more money. This general rule goes for all lenders making any kind of a get out of foreclosure loan.

The lender must be concerned about the owner going into bankruptcy. A bankruptcy would wipe out a lot of the equity due to the fact the owner does not pay the loan payments during the bankruptcy stalling period, possibly in some cases a year or more. Then there are court costs and attorney fees. Also, an equity lender does not want to be accused of lending too much to encourage a future foreclosure, so that it looks like the lender did it on purpose to gain financially from their own foreclosure.

This leaves the owner in foreclosure searching for a friend, relative, or company to lend the money needed to cure the foreclosure. If these sources are not forthcoming, the owner will suffer a give-away sale for pennies on a dollar or will go to a forced sale by the lender at auction. Either way, the owner's equity in the property is lost. This foreclosure situation repeatedly occurs for owners without a personal money answer. The owner has substantial equity with no way to save it! The owner needs the LP/EFT to provide the money needed to save their property equity.

A BETTER PROPERTY OWNER ANSWER

The LP/EFT is a positive solution that will rescue "all" of the property equity from a pending foreclosure for the owner. The LP/EFT arranges a fresh financial start for the owners by turning the currently financial insolvent owners into qualified cash investors. The LP investment capital gathered from rescuing property equities is invested for the benefit of the property owners. The LP earns a profit for the owner and grows the owner's rescued equity amount.

The LP/EFT helps the owner from incurring harsh costs over the long-term because of the credit problem a concluded foreclosure would cause. Any loan balance, tax, or legal problem a foreclosure would cause is completely and totally avoided by the owner.

The LP/EFT is a welcome answer for the millions and millions of property owners who will face foreclosure in the coming years. It will help property owners, lenders, and real estate professionals gain substantial benefits because it introduces a new and better way to solve a pending foreclosure and to invest safely. This new avenue is sorely needed and has been created to help people and businesses in need of a fair and just answer to the foreclosure problem.

THE OWNER'S COMMITMENT IN THE LP/EFT

The owner agrees to:
- Sell the property through the LP.
- Invest the rescued equity in the LP.
- While in the LP allow their equity rescued to be used to operate and invest.
- Pay loan payments until a property is sold by the LP, if possible.
- No CI will invest to rescue property equity for the benefit of the owner without an appropriate amount of collateral as security. The owner agrees to provide the property title as the necessary collateral.
- The owner agrees to lose the property ownership and the equity, if the property does not sell in the open market. The owner agrees to give the property ownership to the CI, if it becomes necessary.

The Owner Receives:
- In return for the owner's cooperation the LP/EFT provides a lot.
- The foreclosure is cured.
- A high risk legal and financial foreclosure position is solved.
- The LP rescues 100% of the property equity from foreclosure for the owner.
- All the very serious negative consequences of a foreclosure are eliminated.
- The owner gains financial and legal stability with time to reestablish credit.
- The owner is made into a qualified cash investor in the LP upon joining.
- A share of profit grows the owner's rescued equity and gains purchasing power.
- Monthly payments are eliminated, and total property loan balance is paid off.
- The owner can stay in the property until it is sold.
- Owner gets money to move and pay a startup rent, if necessary.
- Owner avoids any potential lawsuit and avoids a long-term credit problem.
- The owner does not pay a dime for the plan and the professional he provided.

The Owners Cost

The owner cost to cure the foreclosure and sell the property comes initially from the CI's invested amount in the LP, the funds used are reimbursed out of the property proceeds when the property sells. The standard cost of sale is paid by the owner out of the property equity when the property sells.

The owner's costs are as follows calculated to be pay from property sales:

♦ Pays for three professional property reports.

♦ Pays the money to reinstate the property default.

♦ Pays cost to fix up the property to sell.

♦ Pay sale and closing costs.

Question? What is the owner's cost of not joining! In the final analysis, the LP pays the CI $25,500 Bonus for the owner. Image having someone pay for you to rescue your money!

WOULD THE OWNER IN FORECLOSURE JOIN

Question: Would you join the LP/EFT to cure a foreclosure, if you were about to lose all your equity and suffer severe financial consequences for many years to come? Or would you rather rescue all your equity, avoid foreclosure, and grow your equity in a LP? Most owners will join to help themselves out of a terrible financial jam. The LP/EFT gives the owner a choice that would be difficult to refuse! The owner in foreclosure is faced with a serious problem! The owner must join the LP/EFT or suffer a serious financial consequence that a foreclosure auction or a give-away sale would cause.

By joining, the owner becomes a qualified investor in an LP and saves and grows their equity capital while simultaneously avoiding all the long-term negative consequences of foreclosure. The owner joining the LP can attract the necessary money and time to restructure his current negative financial standing and build a strong financial future. The owner can now rescue their entire financial nest egg, which is represented by the equity in their property, that they are counting on for their future security. The owner gets a fresh financial start and avoids having to start over again with no credit or money.

HOW THE OWNER JOINS THE /EFT

Step 1

The owner reviews a Preliminary Understand and agrees to the terms offered. (note: no legal contract is made at this point)

Step 2

The owner arranges for 3 professional reports on the property for the prospective CI to analyze and decide to invest. An Appraisal Report, a Contractor Report and a Preliminary Title Report are provided by the owner.

Step 3

The owner waits until the CI approves the property using the three professional reports to do so. The GP of the LP must also approve the reports.

Step 4

Upon approval of the property by the CI and GP the owner signs the Articles of Partnership and deposits the property Bare Title into the escrow handling the LP, simultaneously. (The Articles are the only legal binding contract between the parties.)

Step 5

The owner becomes a qualified "cash investor" when the LP cures the foreclosure and sells the property at a fair market price. The rescued equity acts as the owner's investment capital in the LP.

Step 6

The owner waits for the LP to invest the funds. Depending on which date the owner joins, the owner could be in the LP for up to a maximum of eight years. The LP operates for eight years from the date of inception unless the partners want to extend the time.

Step 7

The owner receives a share of the LP net profit, and the rescued equity (capital invested) is returned in full.

HONESTY AND DOING IT THE RIGHT WAY

- ♦ Scamming the owner in foreclosure makes the word foreclosure a nasty word. The state and federal foreclosure laws that control "negative foreclosure actions", by unscrupulous cheats, do not apply to the activity of the LP/EFT because the LP/EFT financially helps the owners a great deal!
- ♦ The LP/EFT solves the foreclosure, rescues all the equity entirely for the owner's benefit, and pays the CI a 42.5% Bonus for and on behalf of the owner out of LP gross investment profit earned.
- ♦ No owner money is ever taken from the owner by the CI or the LP/EFT.
- ♦ The owner is free of any cost!
- ♦ LP/EFT works to educate and improve what happens to an uneducated first-time troubled owner in the foreclosure process.
- ♦ In the LP the owner, the CI, and the LP are all recipients of financial benefits of the LP/EFT.
- ♦ That is what is important, everyone wins!

PART THREE
SECURED CASH INVESTOR (CI) SECTION

AN ORIGINAL SECURED CI POSITION

An original legal and financial position for a secured CI has been developed in the LP/EFT that features a highly collateralized secured position. The CI structure is anchored in legal, financial and investment principals that protect and reward the CI in unique and valuable ways! The low-risk high-return combination affords the CI an investment position that is extremely hard to equal.

This investment deals with both the property owner in foreclosure turned into a cash investor in the LP/EFT and a secured CI position. The LP/EFT introduces an exceptional safe and rewarding investment structure and procedure for both. In the LP/EFT the CI is backed with substantial collateral that protects against loss. The CI capital is secured, has a new investment arrangement, a different legal structure, and is an investment system advancement. The LP/EFT has established a very safe, legally strong, and highly rewarding investment CI position.

CI INVESTMENT PURPOSE

The reason a CI invests safely in a secured transaction is to earn the highest return possible in the shortest amount of time with no problems! This statement describes and coincides with what happens in the LP/EFT. The CI earns a fixed Bonus payment equal to 42.5% of the capital invested for providing the seed money to start a LP. This seed money invested by the CI is called the Critical Cash Capital (CCC) in the LP and creates a Financial Support Plan in the LP to ensure that the property does not go back into foreclosure. The CI fund invested pays the Notice of Default late payment demand and takes the property out of foreclosure. The CCC also creates selling time to rescue the equity by supporting the loan payment only, if necessary.

New is a different way to pay the secured CI. A pre-agreed fixed amount as the CI Bonus is agreed to up front and is paid in approximately one year. The Bonus reward is a minimum of $25,500 to a maximum of $42,500 for the CI. A small amount from each person in a group of cash investors can invest a minimum of $60,000 up to $100,000 or one investor can invest a single amount.

THE CI HAS A SAFE AND REWARDING INVESTMENT

The CI in the LP/EFT is safe and secured financially and legally with two types of collateral, LP reserve cash from property sales acts as collateral and a "foreclosure free" fee property title of ownership. The reward is $25,500 or higher with no dependence on earning venture profit to collect, the timing to collect is approximately one year, the amount of the reward can grow rapidly with exclusive repeat opportunities and, the initial amount of collateral increases after the investment has started. It is an expense free investment, there is no legal or management responsibility for the investor. There is now an original method to foreclosure investing that is much safer and rewarding than the normal method used in the marketplace by investors today.

The Cash Investor has a very strong industry leading low-risk high-reward investment in the LP Extraordinary Foreclosure Transaction that outperforms other real estate investments in very significant ways. It is an investment position for the cash investor that is very hard (if not impossible) to match in any other real estate investment.

CI POSITION

Legally the limited partners are kept separate so a qualified CI can invest in the same LP with a currently financially insolvent property owner! The CI has his/her own limited partner legal, financial and investment arrangement in the LP. The CI has a position in the LP that has no legal or financial entanglement or reliance on other limited partners.

Every CI wants to make an investment that is secured with the fewest problems possible in the shortest time and that earns a substantial reward.

This LP/EFT does exactly that for the CI!
1. The CI is secured with substantial collateral.
2. The CI reward is a fixed amount of $25,500 or higher.
3. The timing to collect the reward is approximately one year.
4. The reward can grow in amount and be completed quicker with repeat opportunities.
5. The investment is an expense free for the CI.

and for the CI:
✓ There is no legal or management responsibility.
✓ There is no need for cash reserves ever.
✓ There is no foreclosure or bankruptcy possible.
✓ There is no monthly payment problem.
✓ There is no legal collection problem.
✓ There is no property trashing concern.
✓ There is no owner move out problem.

PROPERTY AS COLLATERAL
1) The amount of initial collateral is established by the CI approving a property that will be taken out of foreclosure.

2) The foreclosure free property ownership with substantial equity is pledged to the CI as the collateral.
3) The CI in the LP has a dual collateral arrangement.
4) The CI security goes up because of the Priority Use Position (PUP), it requires all LP cash on hand to be used before CI funds can be expended.
5) The collateral amount increases with each LP property sale that happens.
6) The risk goes down with each LP operating cash fusion from a LP property sale.

CI LEGAL POSITIONS ARE ESTABLISHED

- The CI has two legal positions as a limited partner in the LP. The "Articles of Partnership" and a "Performance Trust Deed" both have legal standing that secure and protect the CI.
- The CI funds invested has a Priority Use Position (PUP) over all LP cash on hand and the CI funds can only be spent after all LP cash is first expended.
- The CI has a right to receive a Grant Deed transferring the property's Absolute Ownership from the LP, if it becomes necessary.
- The CI will own the property only if the LP exhausts all the CI funds without selling the property! The collection of the title is immediate as the LP is legally required to transfer the title, if it becomes necessary.
- It is important to realize that the control of what happens in the LP is agreed to through agreement in the Articles of Partnership. The terms and conditions are agreed to before the Articles are signed. After the Articles are signed the LP legally starts and the limited partners have no management in the LP.

CI OCCURENCES

- The one and only act of the CI is to invest capital to financially start-up the LP.
- The CI invests LP start-up funds in return for a reward in the form of a Bonus.
- The CI is an investor in name only, as the CI does not participate in any risk investment for profit made by the LP.
- The property title of ownership, taken out of foreclosure by the LP, is the collateral pledged to secure the CI start-up funds.
- The CI is only investing start-up funds secured with "a pledge" of an absolute fee ownership of property title with substantial equity approved by the CI.
- The LP using the CI funds invested will afford owners, in dire need of a financial help, a fair and honest answer to their foreclosure problem.
- The owner's purpose in transferring the property's Bare Title to the LP is to have the property fee ownership pledged as collateral to the CI, to attract and secure investment capital.

- Upon the Grant Deed "Bare Title" transfer to the LP owner is fulfilling a condition laid down in the Articles of Partnership.
- A new fast and better collateral "collection method" is designed for the CI.
- There is no legal or management responsibility, there is no need for cash reserves ever, there is no foreclosure or bankruptcy involvement possible, and there is no time delay or expensive legal collection problem for the CI in the LP/EFT.

A NEW CI BONUS REWARD SYSTEM

- The Bonus is a pre-agreed 42.5% of the amount of capital and it is a fixed amount that cannot go up or down.
- Within the LP a new method, the use of a PTD, ensure the Bonus payment promised and return of the CI investment capital is made.
- A LP Bonus payment that pays a CI a pre-agreed Bonus equal to 42.5% of the capital invested by the CI, is paid from of the net sales proceeds the third property sale.
- Forty-two and one-half percent (42.5%) of $60,000 invested by the CI equals a Bonus of $25,500. The Bonus can be a minimum of $25,500 to a maximum of $42,500.
- A small investment amount by each member in a group to arrive at a minimum of $60,000 is one way to accumulate the minimum amount, or in a single amount up to $100,000 by one person can be invested.
- The Bonus is secured by a PTD that is recorded by the escrow against the property being used as the collateral for the CI invested funds.
- The LP has a different and much better way to pay the CI with a cash Bonus reward. The 42.5% is not an interest rate or rate of return, it is a lump sum Bonus payment for a one-time act of providing start-up funds (seed money) to the LP.
- There is no dependence on the LP having to earn profit to pay the Bonus to the CI. The CI pre-agreed Bonus is earned in an extraordinarily safe way!
- The LP pays the CI $25,500 Bonus. The LP agrees to reimburse the owner's capital account the funds used from property sales to pay the CI Bonus. The funds to reimburse the owners' capital accounts will come out of the gross profits earned from LP investments.
- The Bonus is earned immediately when the CI puts funds into escrow, and the Bonus is paid to the CI out of the third LP sale.
- The estimated Bonus timing is based on the time it takes to sell three LP properties. The timing for the CI to collect the Bonus is approximately one year.
- The Bonus growth can be accelerated by the CI contracting with the general partner in advance to turn-over funds to invest in an agreed number of LP's.

CI RECEIVES A PERFORMANCE TRUST DEED

A Performance Deed of Trust (PTD) secures the collateral (a property ownership title) given to the CI, if necessary. The equity amount in the collateral property being held for sale by the LP is maintain and cannot go down. The LP Articles of Partnership coupled with a Performance Trust Deed working together cause an CI to be legally secured in a new and safe way.

The PTD type of investment arrangement is much stronger than just having a normal trust deed securing a property equity. This legal PTD position is arranged in the LP Articles of Partnership. It gives the CI the legal control the CI wants through the Articles of Partnership to guarantee the collateral collection that protects CI funds.

THE PERFORMANCE TRUST DEED

The LP introduces an exceptional safe and rewarding investment structure and procedure for a CI. Substantial collateral, a new financial technique and a different legal design all together establish a strong and highly rewarding CI position. The CI has two legal contractual standings in the investment, the Articles and the PTD, that together maximizes safety and ensures the reward collection. These first-time financial and legal advantages together establish a very safe and profitable investment scenario!

The CI receives a "Performance Trust Deed" (PTD) that secures the collateral "pledged" in a way that has never been arranged before in a LP. The "Performance Trust Deed" advantages for the CI are many. The safety, reward and timing differences between regular trust deed investing and this Performance Trust Deed way of investing are very significant and are very attractive, secure and rewarding.

Earning Improvement
Standard Deed of Trust Investment:

Results vary in regular trust deed investing from single to double-digit returns, because of negative variables that could occur. The return amount is unknown until completion.[SEP]

Major Distinction:[SEP]

This new Trust Deed way offers a pre-agreed, fixed amount of $25,500 up to $42,500 in approximately one year. The same potential negative variables that occur in a regular trust deed investment are not possible in the PTD investment.

Collateral Improvement
Standard Deed of Trust Investment:

If the owner does not pay the monthly payments the property equity total can diminish the collateral by the amount not paid very rapidly. A foreclosure also lowers the collateral amount, and if started becomes a serious time, money and legal problem for the investor.

Major Distinction:

The collateral given to the CI exceeds by far the amount that a typical trust deed Investment offers and cannot diminish. There is no foreclosure possible.

Investment Time Improvement

Standard Deed of Trust Investment:

The average length of a loan secured by a trust deed is three to five years. sep

Major Distinction: sep

This Trust Deed investment timing is approximately one (1) year. The timing can be shortened even further with repeat investment and would also increases the amount of the CI reward.

Foreclosure Bankruptcy Improvement

Standard Deed of Trust Investment:

The borrower's nonpayment creates legal problems such as foreclosure or bankruptcy that are costly time consuming and can severely diminish the CI's bottom line.

Major Distinction:

In this CI PTD legal scenario, a foreclosure or bankruptcy that would cost the CI time and money cannot happen.

CI ADVANTAGES ACHIEVE A LOW-RISK INVESTOR POSITION

- The CI Invests in a secured transaction in a LP as a limited partner while other limited partners are not secured!
- The CI Invests in an investment that is fully funded at the very start and there will be no need for additional capital from the CI ever!
- The CI is privileged by a system within the LP that provides dual collateral for the CI investment. The LP cash-on-hand and the pledge of the absolute property ownership both act as collateral to protect the CI funds!
- The CI is paid with a new payment system in a limited partnership. The Bonus is paid out of existing property sold for the owner by the LP.
- The CI Collateral in the LP increases with each LP property sale because of the Priority Use Position (PUP) granted to the CI in the Articles of Partnership! All cash on hand must be expended by the LP according to the PUP before the CI fund money is used by the LP for any reason including to take in new foreclosure properties.

- The CI is paid a pre-agreed fixed percentage of 42.5% of the capital invested as a Bonus. The collateral (a foreclosure free property ownership) offered to the CI should have enough remaining equity to secure the Bonus as well as the CI capital invested! The <u>Bonus is a fixed percent rate</u> and is not an interest rate or rate of return on capital!
- The CI is <u>not involved in any risky profit-making venture</u> of the LP. The CI Bonus is earned immediately for funding the $60,000 and is paid when the LP makes three property sales.
- The CI is privileged with a <u>quick return of capital</u> after three LP property sales are made, estimated to take one year or less!

CI LEGAL POSITION IS STRONG

The CI has contracted for terms and conditions designed to complete the intentions of the CI in the LP Articles of Partnership. The CI is making a secured trust deed investment in a unique, very safe and rewarding way in the LP. The CI receives a legal binding Performance Trust Deed that creates a second legal position, the first being the LP Articles of Partnership. These two legal standings in the same investment for the CI means there are two legal avenues for the CI to collect the return of capital. The CI has a Trust Deed investment with extraordinary legal safeguards not found in normal trust deed investment. And:

- The CI funds are safe and secure with two types of collateral.
- The CI has two different legal standings in the LP investment.
- The CI reward is fixed at $25,500 or higher.
- The CI timing to collect is approximately one year.
- The CI reward can grow rapidly with repeat opportunities.
- The CI initial collateral increases after the investment starts.
- The CI has an expense free investment.
- The CI has no legal or management responsibility.
- The LP/EFT affords the CI a low-risk coupled with a high-return investment that
- completes in approximately 1 year and pays $25,500 or more!

NEW GROUNDBREAKING RISK VS REWARD COMBINATION

Whenever an CI makes an investment choice, the main consideration in making the choice is the RISK VS REWARD status of the investment. There are not many different risk vs reward opportunities to choose from, they all imitate one another. The LP/EFT low-risk and high-return combination adds up to a very attractive investment, one that would be very difficult to equal.

In investing it is either:

A Low Risk--Low Return Opportunity

Or

A High Risk--High Return Opportunity

(Big Time Gambling)

The LP/EFT Investment offers a new choice:

➥**A LOW RISK-HIGH RETURN OPPORTUNITY**

CI INVESTMENT QUESTIONS AND ANSWERS

- ◆ Investment amount required?
  ($3,000 in a group of investors or a single minimum of $60,000)
- ◆ How much is paid to the CI?
  (Pre-agreed fixed Bonus of $25,500 up to $42,500 paid to CI)
- ◆ Collateral type and amount?
  (Approved property by CI, equity will exceed capital amount invested)
- ◆ CI Security?
  (Performance Trust Deed secures property fee ownership as collateral)
- ◆ Timing of investment?
  (Flexible estimated one year.)
- ◆ Source of reward?
  (Paid out of real estate property when sold)
- ◆ Reinvestment opportunity?
  (Repeat investment safer and more rewarding)
- ◆ Personal management?
  (CI not involved in management and no legal liability)
- ◆ Investment manager?
  (Corporation)

ELEMENTARY CI QUESTIONS AND ANSWERS

The CI has his/her own limited partner legal, financial and investment arrangement in the LP. There are two classes of limited partners in the LP. The financially qualified CI partner must enjoy and does have substantial collateral as security for the funds invested while having no legal or financially entanglements of any kind with the financially troubled partners in the LP.

The CI must be legally and financially separated from other partners with different obligations, responsibilities, and a different high reward in the LP to make the investment safe and attractive.

The CI has no legal liability for any LP operation and has a high reward in quick time with no managerial involvement. The LP provides the safest investment position ever designed in a LP for a CI to make the investment acceptable and rewarding.

Every CI wants to make an investment that is secured with the fewest problems possible in the shortest time and that earns a substantial reward. This LP does exactly that for the CI!

THE CI INVESTMENTS CONCERNS ANSWERED
The CI

Must be legally kept separate by creating two classes of limited partners so a qualified CI can invest in the same LP with a currently insolvent property investor! The CI has his/her own limited partner legal standing, financial commitment, and investment structure in the LP. The CI has a separate class position that has no legal or financial entanglement with other financially insolvent limited partners. The two classes are completely different from one another and have different reasons for investing, different contributions, different legal and financial standings, different degree of risk, different system of reward, and different timing.

THE CI

Must be financially separate and protected from the financially insolvent property owner in the LP. A Performance Trust Deed (PTD) secures the pledge of property ownership as collateral and makes the CI investment into a secured Trust Deed Investment. This is a separate legal standing from the Articles of Partnership Agreement. Both the PTD and the Articles of Partnership are individual legal rights and have different legal standing!

THE CI

Must be in a secured investment position all the time. The CI invested funds are never without collateral as the Bare Title to the property is deposited to the LP into escrow before the CI deposits Sixty Thousand Dollars ($60,000). The collateral for the CI investment funds is secured with a conditional pledge of fee simple ownership of property to the CI. The CI investment is secured with two types of collateral. The LP cash-on-hand acts as collateral because of the Priority Use Position (PUP) granted to the CI and secondly the property pledge of ownership is also collateral. The amount of the cash-on-hand acting as collateral increases with each LP property sale.

THE CI

Must be free of the "financially insolvent property CI limited partner" having to perform or direct anything in any way for the LP. The General Partner alone has Power of Attorney in the Articles of Partnership and is authorized for making all LP operating decisions.

THE CI

Must be favored with legal, financial and investment advantages over other financially insolvent limited partners in the LP. The CI is granted these legal positions that operate for the first time in a LP.

- ♦ A Limited Partner Contractual Position in the AP.
- ♦ A Performance Trust Deed Position
- ♦ A Priority Use Position (PUP)
- ♦ A Grant Deed Right on condition position
- ♦ A Dual Legal Position to secured and collect collateral

THE CI

Must be extra safe. In a limited partnership it is a fact that the limited partner is legally limited to losing only their capital. However, in the case of the CI the loss of capital means the CI gains a fee simple title of ownership to the property acting as collateral. CI has no foreclosure, bankruptcy, legal responsibility or personal management concerns in the LP.

THE CI

Must be paid on a different basis. A pre-agreed fixed amount secured Bonus is initially paid out of funds from the owner's property sales. The LP then repays the Bonus as an operating expense out of gross profits earned from its investments. There is no dependence on the LP having to earn profit for the CI to collect the Bonus. The CI Bonus is 42.5% of the capital invested by the CI or $25,500 for $60,000 invested. The Bonus can accelerate and increase in amount by reinvesting the original $60,000 and the Bonus together. The timing to collect the Bonus is approximately one year.

THE CI

Must be legally insulated. There is no foreclosure or bankruptcy possible for the CI to be involved in. The LP is required under the Articles of Partnership Agreement to pass the title to the CI if the CI funds are exhausted without a sale occurring. The CI has the Articles of Partnership Agreement and the PTD to claim and collect the title to the property through the court. The claim is based on the agreement spelled out in the Articles that says the property title is conditioned on a certain event occurring.

THE CI

Must not be concerned with the General Partner performance. The subject property in foreclosure is taken into escrow and is cured by escrow. It is then listed for sale by the LP with a qualified broker. As far as the CI is concerned it is a simple property in and property out transaction completed by real estate professionals! The owners in the LP must be concerned, because the LP GP makes all investment decisions using their invested capital!

THE CI

Must be free of any LP management. There is no requirement for any limited partner to perform any management task in the LP. Limited Partnership law requires that no limited partner shall have any management responsibility.

THE CI

Must be able to make an investment that is secured with the fewest problems possible in the shortest time and that earns a substantial reward. LP does exactly that for the CI!

CI NEVER WOULD INVEST UNLESS

Would anyone be an investment partner with a financially insolvent property owner whose property is in the foreclosure process and has little or no money and no credit? The answer is of course no! Not unless of course all the investment concerns of the CI can be eliminated by legally and financially keeping the insolvent limited partners separate from the CI's position in every necessary way.

THE LP/EFT IS A DIFFERENT WAY TO INVEST!

The LP/EFT is like a standard everyday looking real estate transaction in that there is a buyer, seller, and transfer of property when it is completed. However, there is a special challenge for the LP to solve a foreclosure that involves more than just doing a standard buy-sell transaction.

A LP/EFT general overview:
- The LP finds a qualified property in foreclosure.
- The LP CI approves the property to secure invested funds.
- The owner, CI, and GP enter the LP Articles of Partnership.
- The owner transfers the Bare Title to the LP (no cash transaction).
- The CI invests cash into the LP as a limited partner.
- The property taken out of foreclosure is sold by the LP through a broker.

- The LP CI leaves the LP after three sales have been completed by the LP.
- The LP continues by itself to take in more properties in foreclosure.

The has a very different legal, financial, and investment structures. The structure in the LP has a different legal arrangement of several existing legal statutes and regulations. Together in a "new legal formation", there is original way to solve a serious foreclosure financial problem in a better and honest way! The grouping of these legal statutes in a new alinement is what creates a way to process a long sought-after solution to foreclosure.

The first thing that must be realized is that in the LP/EFT the investor is at very low risk. Why because the investor is secured with a pledge of a fee absolute ownership title of a property "free of foreclosure". The property chosen by the investor has an equity amount that is substantially more than the amount invested by the investor. There is a LP plan designed to make sure the payments are made on time. The property equity position does go up with on time monthly loan payments.

The limited partnership financial support plan makes sure that the monthly payments on the property loan(s) are paid on time. This plan prevents the property from going back into foreclosure once it is cured of the foreclosure by the LP. The LP has a legal responsibility to transfer the absolute fee title to the property to the investor if the financial fund (the investors cash invested) in the LP is exhausted supporting the property for sale. In the LP there is no bankruptcy possible involving the cash investor as the title must be transferred to the cash investor.

The collateral guarantee of title by the LP given to the CI is secured with a Performance Trust Deed. As important as the PTD is the Articles of Partnership, which is a legal binding contract, also grants and supports the CI collateral position. These legal positions are legal standings to collect the collateral offered to the investor, if necessary. Two such powerful legal standings as these in the same investment are highly unusual.

CI INVESTMENT POINTS

Nothing has ever been devised that allows an CI to invest safely in a way that helps an owner in foreclosure rescue all their property equity for themselves, until the LP/EFT. A combination of newly generated factors in the LP creates a unique and safe way for the CI to participate in helping people rescue their equity. The LP/EFT investment is safe and earns a substantial reward at the same time.

- CI has a secured investment.
- Articles of the LP control what happens, owners have no say in the LP activity.

- The LP investments are not profit-making ventures for the CI.
- Collateral increases with each property sale and the LP must use its operating funds from property sales first before any the CI investment fund is spent.
- Pre-agreed fix-amount of Bonus cannot go up or down in amount.
- Two chances to succeed for the CI, CI gets Bonus or property.
- CI Acceleration opportunity with a turnover contract.

CI STANDING IN THE LP
- Very low legal, financial, investment risk for the CI in the LP.
- CI Low risk because of legal standing and the funds are secured.
- Shared CI capital funding allows for any amount to be invested.
- CI has a high fixed amount of Bonus.
- CI has quick timing approximately than one year to collect Bonus.
- No LP profit performance required to pay the Bonus.
- CI has no LP legal responsibility.
- CI has no LP management requirement.
- Quick CI reinvestment accelerates earnings.

NORMAL REAL ESTATE JUNIOR LOAN TRANSACTION

To understand a detailed overview of the Extraordinary Foreclosure Transaction it would be very helpful to review an ordinary junior trust deed investment. The difference between the two brings understanding how one is much better than the other. They are very, very different from one another.

In the junior trust deed loan transaction, only the equity in the property is the collateral securing the loan. The equity can overtime go down in amount if the current owner does not pay the monthly payment on both the first and second loan. The investor relies on the owner of the property to make payments on the loans. If the owner fails to pay the monthly payments the equity position is reduced. In the LP loan payments are pre-arranged and are paid on time.

The junior loan lender will have to make up the payments not made on the first loan balance that were not made by the owner. This is required for the investor to legally foreclose on the property to gain the ownership of the property to sell to recoup the funds loaned. Now the investor has obtained the ownership of the property after foreclosing and must support the first loan payment and maintain the condition of the property with additional money.

Making up the late payments, fixing up the property for sale, supporting the property first payments until it sells, paying all related costs of foreclosing until the property sells financially destroys the invested result intended.

Bankruptcy is another serious problem for the junior loan lender because a bankruptcy can take years to be concluded. Maintenance of the property may be a problem if the owner did not leave the property in good physical condition, and this must be fixed with more money to sell the property at full price. For the investor money after more money is necessary to collect back the original loan amount. None of these negative money events can happen in the LP!

If everything goes right for the junior loan lender in a normal trust deed investment that's great. A normal 12% profit is considered excellent. However, the lender has got to keep his fingers crossed and hope for the best. No crossing fingers when investing in the LP/EFT is necessary, the return is much higher, and no addition investor money will ever be needed for any reason!

COMPARING THE CI INVESTMENT TO A JUNIOR LIEN LOAN

Investing general considerations are risk, reward, timing, legal concerns, management. When a junior loan investment is compared to the LP/EFT investment, the comparison makes it clear that the LP/EFT investment stands head and shoulders over the junior lien loan investment.

JUNIOR LOAN PROBLEMS
2nd Loan Lender Concerns/Problems:
♦ First loan default by owner, after curing default with new 2nd loan.
♦ May need to start foreclosure as second holder to protect money lent.
♦ Loan payment must be made to 1st lender by 2nd lender while 2nd forecloses.
♦ Potential Bankruptcy from owner/borrower to stall foreclosure.
♦ Owner may trash the property before leaving the property.
♦ Refurbish cost to prepare for sale.
2nd Loan Risk
♦ Betting on financially strapped owners' financial performance.
♦ Time in question because of another owner default.
♦ Amount of earning can vary and is in always in question.
2nd Loan Reward
♦ Varies based on performance.
♦ Usually,10% or more with good performance.

- 2nd Loan Timing
- Usually, 3 to 5 years. If there is a default timing can change.

CI ADVANTAGES OVER JUNIOR 2ND LOAN
LP/EFT Details
- Fixed amount of Bonus at 42.5% of capital invested.
- Ownership Is Collateral.
- Ownership of the property stands as collateral.
- Collateral is the title to the property with equity that can only increase.
- Payments are made by the LP to ensure CI of full equity amount.
- Legal Position.
- No CI bankruptcy or foreclosure involvement is possible.
- CI has two legal positions to collect title in case of default, if necessary.
- Articles of Partnership
- Performance Trust Deed Timing
- Property Ownership
- If CI ends up owning property, the full equity position has been maintained.
- The property has been kept up by the owner to achieve a full sale.
- All property will sell for an appraised value if marketed by a professional within a reasonable time!
- Three property sales will take approximately 1 year

THE CI KNOWS
- The LP property taken out of foreclosure will be put up for sale immediately.
- There is a Financial Support Plan to financially support the property until sale.
- That net sales proceeds from LP properties pay the Bonus.
- That the funds from the properties sold by the LP are used to pay the Bonus and replaced from future LP gross profits.
- The owner has a strong interest in maintaining value of the property.
- That there will be no need for more CI cash to protect the original cash invested.
- That the CI knows exactly what the CI invested funds are limited to be spent on.
- Ahead of time the CI knows the exact amount of the Bonus.
- The CI collateral amount will increase after each LP sale.
- The up-to-date appraised value of the property establishes the collateral.
- The CI funds will be returned in full before any LP investing for profit begins.
- The legal and financial positions of the CI are separate from other partners.
- If the owner pays the full loan payment on time the LP will not have to use any portion of the funds invested by the CI to make the payment.

- That the LP partners do not control the money invested by the CI or the property title, nor are they able to make any LP decisions.
- There can be no bankruptcy by the LP, the LP must turnover the title to the CI according to the Articles of Partnership.

CI PRECEDURE TO JOIN THE LP

Step 1.

The CI reviews a Preliminary Understanding that is not a legal contract. It just explains how the LP works and spells out the terms and conditions of the LP, the roles of owner, and the CI.

Step 2.

The CI reviews three professional reports of a property that deal with the property appraised value, physical condition and legal status. A personal visit is advised!

Step 3.

The CI signs the LP Articles of Partnership, the legal binding agreement that is a behavior blueprint for all partners in the LP.

Step 4.

An escrow is open with a qualified company. First the property owner deposits the Bare Title to the property in foreclosure in favor of the LP. Then only after the escrow receives the owner's Bare Title to property, that is in foreclosure, is a PTD in favor of the CI from the LP put into escrow. Then the CI deposits the $60,000 into the escrow.

Step 5.

The escrow then cures the Notice of Default, and the property is no longer in foreclosure. Then the escrow records the LP Performance Trust Deed for the CI in the land record office against the property. **Note:** the PTD is recorded against a property that is no longer in foreclosure and now the value of the property is once again the real market value. The CI has both a contractual agreement (the Articles) and a Performance Trust Deed as security.

Step 6.

The first property is sold by the LP and any monies used out of the $60,000 invested by the CI to cure the foreclosure is replenished. The CI fund is replenished out of each LP property sale.

Step 7.

The second and third properties are acquired and sold by the LP in the same way as the first property.

Step 8.

The CI leaves the LP after receiving the capital invested and Bonus promised out of the third property sale escrow, in approximately one year.

SIMPLY PUT THE CI INVESTMENT PROCESS

- ◆ Receives a Preliminary Understanding that recites the terms and conditions and how
- ◆ the LP/EFT works for the CI.
- ◆ Approves the first property that starts the LP operating.
- ◆ Signs the LP Articles of Partnership after the owner signs.
- ◆ Becomes an CI in the LP by depositing $60,000 into escrow.
- ◆ Receives a PTD after the property foreclosure is cured.
- ◆ Leaves the LP after three property sales are made.

COMMENTS

The LP/EFT is very different and is not similar in any way to the standard foreclosure investment legal or financial structure. There are several key elements of law used, and specially designed investment strategies introduced in the LP/EFT that provide a brand-new investment opportunity. With the LP/EFT solving a major part of the foreclosure problem for real estate brokers, lenders, bankruptcy courts, property owners and, at the same time providing new job opportunities makes the social value extensive. It is a win-win for everyone involved, especially the property owners across our country.

PART FOUR
LIMITED PARTNERSHIP (LP) SECTION

THE LIMITED PARTNERSHIP (LP).

The Foreclosure Answer Affirmed, Inc (FAA), a Virginia Corporation, has a "finance answer" to a foreclosure problem that features a specially designed Limited Partnership. The LP provides a "financial answer" that allows for a property owner to get out of foreclosure to rescue the remaining property equity!

The LP in concert with an Extraordinary Foreclosure Transaction (EFT) is used to provide and complete the financial answer for the property owner in financial distress. Once the equity is rescued by the LP a real estate brokerage company is used to sell the owner's property, that has been taken out of foreclosure, for the total financial benefit of the owner.

The serious problem of foreclosure is fashioned in cement and will never change. The laws regarding foreclosure are geared to legally recovering the lenders collateral (owner's property) in the case where the loan is defaulted upon. If the loan is defaulted upon the lender must foreclose and sell the property to recoup the funds loaned. The Limited Partnership and the Extraordinary Foreclosure Transaction (LP/EFT) together originate and provide a "financial answer" for the owner to cure the foreclosure and rescue the equity.

THE LP EXTRAORDINARY FORECLOSURE TRANSACTION

There is a buyer, seller, and a limited partnership in the LP. The LP original legal structure is the most intricate and crucial part of the LP. It has new investment and operational techniques that create an ability to perform in a new way. The LP structure, benefits, and collateral position are all original and the legal structure in the LP is unique.

GENERAL PRECEDURE

The EFT is the transaction, and the LP is the legal vehicle that carries out the transaction. The EFT in the LP is a three-party real estate transaction between a property owner in foreclosure, a secured cash investor, and the LP. Each limited partner has an individual purpose, a different legal standing, and special investment position in the LP. The LP features two types of very different cash investors in the same LP, a secured CI and a property owner in foreclosure that is turned into a cash investor with the property sale proceeds rescued from foreclosure. The title is transferred to the LP with no money passing hands between the current owner and the LP. The foreclosure owner contributes property to the LP, as an investment, that will act as collateral to secure the CI invested funds after the foreclosure is cured.

- ♦ The GP finds a qualified property in foreclosure.
- ♦ The CI approves the property to secure invested funds.
- ♦ The owner, CI, and LP enter the LP Articles of Partnership.
- ♦ The property is listed for sale and sold by the LP through a broker.

AND THEN

- ♦ The CI leaves the LP after 3 sales have been completed by the LP.
- ♦ The LP continues by itself using funds from property sales.

The EFT looks like but is not the same as a regular property sale. The EFT is like a standard everyday looking real estate transaction in that there is a buyer, seller, and transfer of property when it is completed. However, there is a special challenge for the LP to solve a foreclosure that involves more than just doing a standard buy-sell transaction.

The LP has a very different legal, financial and investment procedure. The legal structure in the LP is a first-time legal arrangement using existing legal statutes and regulations. Together in a new formation they allow for an original way to solve a serious foreclosure financial problem! The grouping of these legal statutes in a new alinement creates a unique way to process a long sought-after solution. Real estate professionals, property owners and related businesses all benefit from the new solution provided by this new legal revelation.

ORIGINAL FORECLOSURE ANSWER

The desperate need for many thousands of property owners in America to avoid foreclosure and rescue all their property equity has been a very serious crisis for centuries. For the owner who cannot solve a pending foreclosure, the LP has been designed to help rescue the property equity from foreclosure. The LP cures the foreclosure, rescues the equity for the owner, and makes the owner into a qualified cash investor to grow the rescued equity. The special ability to rescue the 100% of the equity and make it grow has never been developed before.

The LP offers a fresh financial start for owners by turning the currently financial insolvent owners into qualified cash investors. The owner's investment capital in the LP is invested and used for the benefit of the property owner rescued from a property foreclosure. The LP pays a profit share to the owner, and this grows the owner's rescued equity amount.

An owner with substantial equity in their property, who is served with a Notice of Default, that the owner cannot cure, is going to lose the equity. The LP has the owner rescuing and investing the equity in an original way. The LP is designed to both solve a financing problem in the foreclosure market, and to raise large sums investment capital in an LP Operating and Investment Fund (O&IF) to invest for the owner's benefit.

A SAFE REWARDING INVESTMENT

Introduced in the LP is a unique financial structure adaptation that creates an exceptionally safe and rewarding investment for a CI. An investment structure advancement in a LP has been developed that is anchored in legal, financial, and investment principles that greatly protect and reward a CI!

The CI funds invested are highly collateralized using a new financial technique and a different legal approach that establishes a strong and highly rewarding investment. The CI capital is secured from the point of commitment to completion and there is no management or legal responsibility for the CI in the LP. The CI is granted new and separate legal positions with major financial advantages that form a first-time investment opportunity! The LP is carefully designed to avoid any CI loss from happening.

LP/EFT PROVIDES SPECIAL RESULTS

The LP/EFT is particularly designed to introduce secured investment funds in a different and better way to cure a Notice of Default, one that the owner could not cure, because the property in foreclosure is highly leveraged and, the property owner is currently financially insolvent. Both the property itself and the owner do not qualify to borrow money needed to cure the Notice of Default. This with as much as twenty-five percent (25%) or more of the property value remaining as equity. However, the LP/EFT provides the necessary funds to help the owner solve the problem.

Major abilities of the LP/EFT:

♦ Rescues 100% of the property equity for the owner and makes it grow substantially, instead of the owner losing all the equity because the owner could not cure the default.

♦ Changes a potential sale under duress by the owner, which amounts to a give-way for pennies-on-the-dollar, because it is in the process of being foreclosed upon, into a sale at "arms-length" that will achieve a full value sale.

♦ Immediately changes a financially insolvent property owner into a qualified "investor" by having the owner use the rescued equity as investment capital, so that the equity can substantially grow in amount and create addition future purchasing power.

43

- Grants the secured CI individual legal positions in the LP/EFT that provides extraordinary legal, financial, and reward protections never offered before to an investor in a real estate transaction. This set of CI protections in the LP/EFT coupled with a "Bonus" payment adds up for the CI to a very safe and rewarding investment!
- Fashions original real estate transactions. The LP/EFT shapes and adjusts ways to operate "standard every day real estate transactions" into improved financial structures that are safer. In addition, there are original transaction designs using the ability achieved from and with the large LP Operating and Investment Fund (O&IF). This large growing O&IF allows for unique investment scenarios to solve many types of financial problems.

LP SALIENT POINTS
What the LP does:
- Introduces investment funds to cure a Notice of Default in a different and better way than has been discovered thus far.
- Provides an owner with a method to rescue the property equity from foreclosure and a way to become a cash investor to grow the equity rescued.
- Creates a very large LP investment fund (O&IF) that will be used to invest in all categories of investment transactions to earn profit for its limited partners.
- Establishes a way to control the sale of a large amount of properties taken out of foreclosure while at the same time being in control of a huge investment fund.
- Fashions original real estate transactions. There are many original operational techniques that fashion unique real estate transactions. This ability comes because of having such a large LP Operating and Investment Fund (O&IF).
- Offers a legal and financial investment arrangement for a secured CI that is second to none. The low-risk high-reward investment position is exceptional for the secured CI, and it would be very hard if not impossible to match.
- The LP is an important revelation with original and exclusive knowledge arranged in a unique order, that results in an ability to rescue property equities from being lost to a foreclosure.
- The LP introduces cash to solve a foreclosure in a unique and safe way for the first time in the real estate industry. It is also the first time that cash and property title act as dual collateral for the CI. This changes the difficult investing decision in the normal foreclosure market into an easy choice to invest in the LP/EFT.
- Sophisticated legal, financial and investment arrangements are introduced in the that bring into play a design that creates the ability to raise an ever-growing never-ending supply of investment capital.

- A revolutionary legal structure is designed and brought into play in the LP Articles of Partnership. This is an advanced legal structure has never been employed in any other real estate transaction. It allows a qualified CI to invest safely on a secured basis and earn a healthy bonus reward in quick time, approximately in one year, for providing the seed money to start the LP operating.

THE CHALLENGE IS MET

The LP has a special challenge to solve a property foreclosure and rescue the owner's equity from loss to foreclosure. To accomplish this, it involves an original method of operating that is exclusive to the LP. The legal structure and procedures are very different and operate in a profoundly original way. The LP has a complete and unique capability to rescue property equity from foreclosure for the owner's benefit.

Within the LP, a new real estate financial approach enters the market. Its methods and operation have never existed before. Under severe financial duress, the owner becomes a qualified CI in a new exclusive arrangement. The entire equity in the property is rescued for the owners and grows with profit share while all the ugly legal and financial consequences of a foreclosure are avoided.

The market is not limited to just the foreclosure market. The LP ability to raise large amounts of operating and investment capital for the LP to invest makes it possible to deal with a wide range of property owners' real estate financing problems. It is not every real estate transaction that has so much to offer as this LP/EFT does.

The LP/EFT answer is not found in any other investment arrangement and is truly a unique development that saves a financial catastrophe from occurring to the owner. All the professional time, talent, and use of the exclusive LP/EFT are cost-free to the property owner. And the Bonus is paid by the LP for the owner.

The LP/EFT addresses in a positive way a large segment of the foreclosure market that has never been approached before in a helpful way. The LP/EFT provides a financial answer to a large part of the foreclosure market and offers a new safe and rewarding secured way to invest.

The LP/EFT arranges financial benefits for property owners, real estate brokers, lenders, and related businesses never offered in any other investment.

There are several key elements of law used, and specially designed investment strategies are introduced in the LP that establish a brand-new investment opportunity.

It is able raise large sums of investment capital that will provide answers for all kinds of real estate financing problems.

Most of all the LP/EFT is an original investment for a secured CI and a financially troubled property owner. The risk-reward status arranged for both original types of investors in the LP is outstanding and sets a new standard for real estate investing.

THE LP IS REALLY NEW
The LP has:
- A self-generating system of raising investment capital.
- A bona fide solution that rescues equity from loss due to foreclosure.
- A secured CI position within a LP.
- A new type of property investor and a new qualified CI position in a LP.
- A protection made for and that favors one secured CI.
- An avenue for owners to recover financially and grow.
- A first-time original investment low-risk high-reward combination.
- A first-time never-before created real estate transaction.

UNDERSTANDING THE LP/EFT
The LP has many individual parts are not complicated. However, there are unique legal, financial and operating structures that covers a lot of material to be learned before the LP/EFT can be understood. If standard investment questions were asked, about how the LP/EFT works without first learning the LP/EFT, the answers would make no sense. Very little of the legal and investment techniques created can be called standard in the LP.
- The categories introduced here:
- The LP structure and operation.
- The CI legal, financial and reward structure.
- The LP legal status structure.
- The property legal title transfer.
- The CI unique investment position advancement.
- The LP financing innovation.
- The new exclusive real estate fees and commissions.
- How the raising of operating and investment capital is achieved.
- How the money to cure the foreclosure is provided.
- How valuable spin off transactions and investments come to light.

UNDERSTANDING THE LP/EFT PROCESS
A general business company and a LP is all that is required to operate the transaction. The LP is not in the "real estate" business per se! The LP is in the business of only "arranging" financing to cure a foreclosure in an original way for the property owner. The

LP provides a "new financial system" that arranges for and allows for a property owner to finance him/herself out of foreclosure to rescue the remaining property equity! No CI funds invested in the LP are used or invested by the LP for its own benefit. No CI money is loaned or paid to anyone by the LP for any reason.

The owner who invests the property in foreclosure has made a capital contribution to the LP in exchange for a limited partner investment position. No property sale to the LP takes place, an exchange for a limited partner position and a right to share LP profit is what the property owner investor receives.

The Bare Title to the property is transferred to the LP by the owner. The LP receives the Bare Title to hold and sell on behalf of the owner, per the Articles of Partnership. Once the Bare Title is transferred to the LP, the LP can transfer title of ownership to a new buyer. No sale is made to the LP, no transfer of an absolute fee ownership is transferred to the LP. The owner does not transfer the equitable rights, the owner retains the equitable rights which includes physical possession.

No money passes hands, no new loan is created, and no existing loan is assumed or taken subject by the LP receiving the property as a capital contribution. No loan law applies because there is no loan involved. Loan and finance laws do not apply because no new loan or financing activity is happening in the LP/EFT.

A local qualified real estate broker will list and sell the property for the LP, after it is taken out of foreclosure. The money from the sale of the property belongs to and is invested in the LP by the property owner rescued from foreclosure. The owner is joining the LP as a limited partner by making a property investment, instead of a cash investment.

The owner retains the current loan responsibility and the title company property insurance stays in place until the property is sold. A new buyer will apply a new property policy from a title company when the property is sold by the LP.

A transfer of property as an investment always qualifies as a tax deferred event. If a property is "invested" and no money is involved, there is an automatic step-up-basis at the start of the investment equal to the appraised value. No tax is due on profit made in the investment until the LP shares profit at the dissolution of the LP, when profit is paid.

THE LP/EFT OPERATION OVERVIEW

The LP can raise large sums of investment capital in an O&IF that will provide answers to all kinds of real estate financing problems, in addition to solving a foreclosure problem. The LP is not limited to just solving foreclosures, it can work on solving any financially troubled property problem. The LP/EFT has an original investment for both a secured CI and a financially troubled property owner. The low-risk high-reward status created for CI sets a new standard in investing.

1. The CI Safety Factors

1a) Dual legal standing means there are two ways to prove and collect the collateral pledge in case of a default by the LP. The Articles of Partnership and the Performance Trust Deed are both a legal avenue to demand in court, the absolute fee title to property held as collateral by the LP for the CI.

1b) The LP GP is legally required by and in the Articles of Partnership to give over the legal title to the property, if the CI funds are totally exhausted by the LP, without a sale of the property being made.

1c) The preliminary title report, the appraisal report and the contractor report are all completed and provided to the CI to help the CI make the investment decision. The CI must approve the property that will act as collateral.

1d) The CI has a conditional right to property ownership title, only if there is a default, created by the fact that the CI's investment funds in the LP were completely exhausted in the effort to sell the property.

2. The LP Legal Structure

2a) The LP legal structure is a first-time ever conglomeration of legal statues and terms designed exclusively to accomplish a certain purpose, that of rescuing property equities from being lost through foreclosure.

3. The CI Timing

3a) The timing for the CI to earn and be paid the Bonus promised by the LP is approximately one year. This of course may vary depending on the sale timing of three LP properties.

4. The CI Bonus

4a) The does not have to earn an investment for profit to pay the CI the Bonus ($25,500) promised. The Bonus is paid from LP gross profits; the CI Bonus is paid by the LP for the benefit of the owner of the property. The Bonus is initially paid from LP property sales contributed by the owners and then replaced from LP gross profits.

4b The owner does not have to pay the CI Bonus ($25,500) for using the CI money to cure the foreclosure. In the final analysis the LP pays the Bonus out of LP investment gross profits.

5. The Amount Of A Pre-Agreed Fixed Amount Bonus.

5a) The amount of Bonus reward promised the CI is calculated in an unusual manner. The amount invested by the CI is multiplied by 42.5% to determine the Bonus. The 42.5% is not an interest rate or rate of return on investment. It merely is a way of calculating a Bonus amount that will be paid to the CI for the sole purpose of providing investment funds to start-up and operate the LP. The Bonus amount is fixed and cannot go up or go down in amount because of normal investment variables.

6. There Is No Management Required Of The CI.

6a) There is no personal management for the CI in the LP. The only thing the CI does is sign off a Performance Trust Deed at the closing of the sale of each property. The CI does this on each of the three properties sold by the LP, one at a time.

7. There Is No Legal Liability For The CI.

7a) In a limited partnership there is no legal liability for the performance of the LP for the limited partners. The General Partner of the partnership is legally and financially responsible for the activity and performance of the partnership itself. The only risk the CI has is the potential loss of the amount of funds invested by the CI, which of course is secured with substantial collateral.

8. There Is A Reinvestment Opportunity.

8a) Once the investment has been successful for the CI and it does very well, it becomes a reason to ask can I reinvest as a CI again and again? The answer is yes you can.

8b) When one Bonus amount reaches the maximum amount ($100,000) that can be invested in a LP, the Bonus can then be split in two to start two LPs at one time.

9. There Is An Exclusive Joint Venture Opportunity For The CI.

9a) As the LP has a responsibility to invest the proceeds from the owners who have rescued their equity from foreclosure, it becomes possible to arrange various types of investments. Joint venturing becomes safer and very rewarding for the CI. The GP of the LP can offer a 50-50 joint venture proposition which is very common, however, the LP can also finance the project with a low interest rate. No bank or financial institution is necessary to borrow from when joint venturing with an LP. Having a partner like this is very advantageous in several ways.

10. The Collateral For The CI Has Been Approved By The CI And It's In An Amount Greater Than The Amount Invested By The CI.

10a) No CI would make an investment that he/she didn't know was substantially and adequately collateralized. So, what is collateral for the CI? There are three reports given to the CI to evaluate the property that is going to act as the collateral. The appraisal report particularly will show the value of the property and the amount owning and the difference will be the collateral amount that the CI will decide on. If the amount to be invested in the LP is less by a substantial amount, then the property's equity amount, then the CI would approve the property to act as collateral.

11. The CI In Earning By Helping Other People In A Very Important Way.

11a) Personal earnings is always the name of the game. However, when the CI knows that the investment being made by him or her is going to really help someone a great deal, it is like receiving a second reward.

12. The CI Has A New Investment Legally And Financially.

12a) Seldom, if ever do you see such a strong dual investment structure such as in the LP . The legal aspects for the CI are outstanding in that the CI has a dual legal standing. Both the LP Articles of Partnership and the Performance Trust Deed protect the CI legally. The financial investment structure is such that either the CI gets a reward as promised or the absolute fee title to an equity rich property.

13. How The CI Protects Him Or Herself By Investing Cash Into The LP.

13a) The Debt to Asset Ratio is improved and makes the investment safe for the CI. The property's equity combined with the cash invested by the CI makes it easier and safer financially for the CI to invest and the LP to operate.

LP/EFT IS A DIFFERENT INVESTMENT
The LP for what it accomplishes is outstanding.

- The LP is specifically designed to operate to cure a pending foreclosure to rescue all the property equity for the owner. The LP has original legal, financial and investment structure incorporated to accomplish the task.
- It has a remarkable investment position arranged for a "secured" limited partner investor. The safety and reward combination are very attractive for the CI and are not equaled in any other type of LP or investment anywhere.
- A new legal and safe investment opportunity with superior advantages is achieved for the LP limited partners. The LP treats each LP partner, the property owner and the CI, with a high degree of respect while offering substantial benefits for both.
- In the LP the CI is offered a dual collateral combination consisting of (1) all LP cash on hand, which increases with every LP property sale per the Priority Use Position (PUP) granted to the CI, and (2) a conditional right to a "foreclosure free" full

property title of ownership. The CI funds are highly collateralized and legally protected. The CI has a very safe investment, regardless that it involves curing a pending foreclosure to start the investment. The LP offers a CI a better way to invest that is very safe, rewarding and timely.

- The CI is every safe because of the strong legal, financial, and reward structures created for the CI, that are without precedent! Between granting the CI dual legal standing that ensures collection of collateral in case of default and growing the collateral amount with LP sales, the CI is as safe as is humanly possible.

- The LP/EFT is not similar in any way to the standard foreclosure investment. There are several key elements of law used, and special investment strategies are introduced for the first time in the LP. It has several original investments, legal, financial and operational techniques. Working together they allow for new abilities and exceptional results.

- The LP has a very different legal, financial, and investment procedures. The legal structure in the LP has a different arrangement using existing legal statutes and regulations. Together in a "new formation," they allow for an original way to solve a serious foreclosure financial problem in a better way! The grouping of these legal statutes in a new alinement is what creates a way to process a long sought-after solution. It opens the door to allow the transaction to operate in a newfound way.

- The LP legal structure is the major "most intricate and critical part" of the LP. It allows new investment and operational abilities that create a greatly improved ability to perform.

- The legal, finance, and investment designs in the LP and EFT are new. These designs for the lender, property owner, and CI, are superior in many ways than is offered in any other limited partnership or real estate investment. Investing in foreclosures and financially troubled real estate property just became a great deal safer and very rewarding by helping other people.

- The LP is organized and operates in a profoundly unique way. The innovative procedure has the same result of a normal property sale. However, it does much more because of what it achieves for the owner, the CI and the foreclosure market. The LP solves a large segment of the foreclosure market that has never been addressed before.

SPECIAL PERFORMANCE

- The LP attributes range a wide financial and investment achievements.
- Rescued all the remaining equity in the owner's property from foreclosure solely for the property owner's benefit.
- Gathered large sums of capital in an LP Operating and Investment Fund for investment, that will grow exponentially, in a never-before conceived method.
- Created an original LP for two types of limited partners who have different purposes and personal qualifications.
- Created an especially safe and rewarding CI position with many legal and financial protections in a LP.
- Secured a CI as a LP limited partner with substantial collateral.
- Created safe investment method for CI to collect a pre-agreed Bonus.
- Created personal income in new and exclusive ways.
- Created operating and investment capital in a profoundly new way.
- Created an original way in a LP to solve a financing problem.
- Provided a money solution for financially troubled properties.
- Established a different system for a foreclosure property owner to invest in.
- Identified a new investment financing system for foreclosure owners.
- Arranged a pledge of a "foreclosure free" fee ownership of a property chosen by the CI as collateral is a first-time occurrence.
- Created a "Operating and Investment Fund" accomplished by rescuing property equities from foreclosure.
- Created a new way to use a Performance Trust Deed to secure a pledge of property ownership.

NEW LP INVESTMENT INNOVATIONS
Here Are Unique Efforts Completed In The LP:

- General Partner takes only Bare Title to the property.
- Rescues equity from being lost to foreclosure in a new way.
- Introduces "secured CI funds" used to cure the foreclosure and rescue the equity.
- Arranges a leading risk-reward scenario for the CI in the LP.
- Makes investing very safe with new legal and investment techniques.
- Arranges two separate contractual positions for the CI.
- Changes a financially insolvent property owner into a "CI" by having the owner use the LP rescued equity as investment capital in the LP.
- Invests and grows the rescued equity for the owner's benefit.
- Cures the foreclosure on the property chosen by the CI.
- Changes a sale under duress of foreclosure that would be a give-a-way for pennies

on the dollar into a "marketplace full value sale" for the owner.
- ♦ Establishes a LP financial support plan to insure property loan payments.
- ♦ Arranges investment capital in the LP and uses it for solutions to various financially troubled properties and new investments.
- ♦ Originates first-time investment transactions and improves standard transactions.

LP first ever innovations:
- ♦ The special secured privilege CI position.
- ♦ The key property owner in foreclosure position.
- ♦ The strong financing structure with many advantages.
- ♦ The investment features a low-risk high-reward position.
- ♦ The improved earning method over other transactions.
- ♦ The quick investment timing opportunity.
- ♦ The safer and more rewarding limited partnership design.
- ♦ The new investment operating techniques.

NEW CI INVESTMENT POSITIONS
- ♦ CI picks and approves property as collateral
- ♦ CI Reward is a pre-agreed fixed up to $42,500.
- ♦ CI timing to collect is approximately one year.
- ♦ CI has an "absolute fee property ownership" as the CI collateral.
- ♦ CI has two legal contractual standings.
- ♦ CI bankruptcy or foreclosure involvement is not possible.
- ♦ CI has normal investment problems under control.
- ♦ CI Has no legal or management responsibility.
- ♦ CI original legal, financial, investment structures create extraordinary safety.

THE LP HAS MANY NEW SYSTEM INVENTIONS
A subset of interesting financial, legal and investment structures and innovations are created. **THEY ARE:**
- ♦ A new structure in a LP for a secured CI.
- ♦ A new real estate investment scenario in a LP.
- ♦ A new CI reward and payment system in a LP.
- ♦ A new innovative collateral system in a LP.
- ♦ A new innovative legal and financial LP structure.
- ♦ A new investment LP scenario for a foreclosure property owner.
- ♦ A new unique LP Performance Trust Deed transaction.
- ♦ A new LP Debt to Asset Ratio original creation.

THE LP/EFT IS AN IMPROVEMENT FOR MANY

For society:

_Solves a serious and difficult foreclosure problem in a fair and just way that society has not been able to solve for centuries.

For businesses:

_Saves money for lending institutions and makes money for other businesses in new expanded ways. Listing and selling properties taken out of foreclosure for full value becomes possible for real estate brokers.

For the CI:

_Creates a better way to invest that is safer, more rewarding, and has a quicker turn-over rate than in other real estate investments.

For CI improved safety:

_Creates a safer legal and financial vehicle for the CI. Creates a first-time method to increase investment collateral for a CI after start of investment.

For property owners:

_Cures legal and financial problems created by a foreclosure. Gives the owners a fresh financial and emotional start. Creates a new investment method for the property owners.

For Lenders

_Cures a default loan and then pays the loan balance off with a property sale.

For the United States government:

_Lowers the number of bankruptcies cases and saves the government money. Creates new type jobs that creates taxable income for the government.

PROFESSIONAL BUSINESSES ALL GAIN

The lenders can now:

♦ Immediately erase a bad loan off the books to reinvest.

The real estate broker can now:

♦ Achieve a "foreclosure free" exclusive listing to sell at full value.

The bankruptcy court can now:

♦ Have a money answer that solves the bankruptcy for the owner, lender and the court.

The qualified CI can now:

♦ Invest with confidence that performance will be very good because advanced legal, financial and investment structures protect the CI.

The attorney can now:

♦ Recommend a real money answer for their clients. Bankruptcy is the only answers the attorney has now!

LOOK AT THE REAL ESTATE BROKER USING THE LP/EFT

Real estate brokers can now associate with a LP/EFT that will have in time many properties for sale over time and each sale will raise substantial operating and investment capital. This combination of having properties for sale and investment capital at the same time allows for unique transactions and investments to be conceived and implemented. **The LP/EFT offers the real estate broker original and valuable abilities.**

- Brokers can now have a "safe" listing of property taken out of the foreclosure process to sell at full value, where it was once was very risky to represent.
- Brokers in new ways earn new type of real estate finder fees and commissions.
- Brokers can now for the first time really help a property owner solve a serious foreclosure problem in a fair and just way by working with the LP/EFT.
- Brokers will have a non-bank source to fund financial problems on all types of properties. The LP/EFT can help any financially troubled property not just property in foreclosure.
- Brokers can now be associated with a LP/EFT that will have in time many different types and priced properties to list for sale. The combination of having several properties for sale and a large investment fund to work with, at the same time, will allow brokers to complete real estate transactions in ways never contemplated before.

PEOPLE AND GOVERNMENT ARE ALL HELP FINANCIALLY

- The CI has a safer and very rewarding investment.
- The Lender is happy to have the foreclosure cured and the principal loan paid.
- The Real Estate Broker is glad to have a foreclosure free exclusive listing with time to attract the full value for the property.
- The CI will have a new joint venture partner opportunity with the LP that will finance the investment.

LP/EFT INVESTMENT DESIGN IS ADVANCED

A real estate CI is always looking for a great investment. An original investment model is created for the CI in this LP. Groundbreaking is a good word to identify the safety, performance, and reward system achieved in this new investment transaction!

The investment does initially involve a property in foreclosure. However, the property foreclosure is immediately cured, and the property enjoys full market value with a substantial equity. A foreclosure free property title of ownership is used to offer as the CI's collateral after the foreclosure is cured. The CI chooses the property that will act as the collateral. The CI is not involved with a property currently in foreclosure, or in a partnership risk type profit-making investment venture of any kind! The LP/EFT is an original, improved, safer way to invest!

The LP investment configuration affords both a property owner in foreclosure and a qualified CI a unique way for each to "safely invest" as limited partners together. It offers a positive solution that will rescue "all" of the property equity from a pending foreclosure for the owner to invest.

LP NEW SAFEGUARDS THE CI
The LP/EFT provides:
- A way for the CI to approve the collateral.
- A way to secure the CI collateral with a property title not just the property equity.
- A way to create CI dual collateral by including all LP cash as collateral.
- A method of increasing the CI collateral through LP sales.
- A way for the CI to check the financial activity of the LP.
- A way for the CI to check the status of the LP collateral.
- A way for the CI to be paid as agreed on time.

SAFETY EVENTS
The LP offers the CI multiple security advantages:
- Real property absolute fee title is the CI collateral.
- Three forms of security for the CI; 1) property title, 2) LP cash reserves, and 3) any loan payments made by the owner also act as funds to protect the CI.
- The CI has two legal standings, the Articles of Partnership and the Performance Trust Deed.
- The CI enjoys a Priority Use Position (PUP) that protects the CI funds invested in the LP. The cash-on-hand increases after the start of the investment with each property sale made and adds to the CI security.
- Pre-agreed fixed amount of Bonus that cannot do up or down in amount.

CI SAFETY FACTS IN THE LP/EFT
- Preliminary title report, Appraisal report, Contractor report.
- A Performance Trust Deed as a legal protection instrument.
- A Conditional grant deed right.
- No foreclosure or bankruptcy concern or expense.
- CI has right to approve first property.
- The CI knows property will be put up for sale immediately.
- LP additional financial resource comes from owner loan payments.
- The owner will leave the property when asked.
- No property maintenance problem.
- Low-risk high-return investment.

- Controlled spending of CI invested funds through Articles Of Partnership.
- CI bonus money not depended on the LP earning a profit.
- CI invested funds are returned out of LP property sales.
- The LP Debt to Asset Ratio receives cash from the CI and it creates less risk.

NEW VALUABLE CI ARRANGEMENTS
In In the LP/EFT these new abilities are all unique CI advantages.
- Created collateral increase and easy collection system.
- Created a special CI Bonus plan.
- Created CI Bonus acceleration plan.
- Created a way to secured only one limited partner.
- Created two chances for the CI to be successful.
- Created new low risk-high reward paradigm.
- Created a secured pledge of property ownership for the CI.
- Created quick timing for the CI.
- Created dual collateral for security.
- Created Bonus payment out of property sales.

THE LP MANY CI SPECIAL INVESTMENT CHARACTERISTICS!
- A new financing advantage.
- A new legal advantage.
- A new safety advantage.
- A new CI reward advantage.
- A new timing advantage.
- A new acceleration advantage.
- A new limited partnership advantage.
- A new investment advantage.

The CI limited partner has his/her own individual limited partner legal and financial position. The "legal structure" has been designed and arranged so that the owners and the CI have different rights, obligations, timing, capital accounts and methods of reward. The two different classes of the investors do not depend upon any performance or promise of each other. This arrangement safeguards the CI and eliminates any legal, financial, investment entanglement of any kind for the CI, with any other currently financially insolvent property owner CI limited partner. Two very different types of investment and legal positions have been created in the same LP.

LP HAS A LOT OF ADVANCEMENTS

- Self-generates operating and investment capital.
- Provides a foreclosure answer.
- The answer for all types of financially troubled property.
- New safety technologies incorporated.
- New exclusive forms of earnings.
- New transaction benefits for the LP, lender, broker, and related businesses.
- All types of property qualify for the LP residential, commercial, apartments, retail, development projects, land, and non-foreclosure financially troubled properties.

CI "CRITICAL CASH CAPITAL" INVESTED IS A "FINANCIAL SUPPORT PLAN"

The CI $60,000 investment in the LP is called "Critical Cash Capital" (CCC). This money creates a "Financial Support Plan" which starts the LP operating and fulfills the initial LP cash requirement.

Financial Support Plan: The money invested by the CI creates a "Financial Support Plan" in the LP . The CI funds are given over on a secured basis to the LP to cure a pending foreclosure on the property. Curing the pending foreclosure restores the property full market value that will act as collateral.

The CCC fund may be used by the LP to financially support the loan payments on the property until it sells. CI cash invested protects the property from going back into foreclosure by paying mortgage payments, if necessary. The liquidity created by the CI cash and the owners making the monthly payment (to the degree they can) are key financial supporting ingredients. This loan payment system maintains and solidifies the full equity position of the property until it is sold.

The $60,000 invested by the CI is used to start the LP.
- Cure the property foreclosure and prepare it for sale.
- Financially support the property until a sale occurs, if necessary.
- Provide for some transaction expenses.
- All CI funds used by the LP is reimbursed out of each property sale.

The CI $60,000 invested creates:
- Money that constructs an acceptable risk in the LP for the CI.
- Money to cure the pending foreclosure.
- Money to establish a LP financial support plan.
- Money independence for the LP by eliminating the need to borrow.
- Money that pays property payments for the owners, if necessary.

- Money changes negotiation under duress to arm's length negotiation.
- Money to fix-up and prepare the property for sale, if necessary.
- Money that encourages the owner to join the LP .
- Money that will allow enough time for the LP to sell the property.

PRIORITY USE POSITION

A "Priority Use Position" (PUP) is granted to the CI in the AOP. The PUP establishes that all the LP cash on hand must be spent before any CI funds invested is spent. This means after the first property sale proceeds come into the LP, some or all the CI funds will now be in reserve which makes the CI position safer. The owner now takes some or all the risk using the funds from the first property sale to take in the next property to sell.

A CI has two types of financial safety positions in the LP. The major collateral position for the CI is the property pledge of absolute fee ownership to the CI. The "Priority Use Position" establishes another second type of security (collateral) in a LP to the great advantage of the CI partner.

LOSS ISSUE

The <u>CI is insulated</u>. In a LP it is a fact that the limited partner is limited to losing the amount invested by law. In the case of the CI losing the capital the CI takes title to a fee absolute ownership of the property offered as collateral, that has a substantial equity position. The LP is required to pass the title of ownership to the CI, if the CI funds are exhausted by the LP without a property sale occurring.

There is no foreclosure or bankruptcy possible for the CI to be involved in that would stall collection of the collateral. The CI has two separate legal documents to exercise the collection of the collateral pledged, the LP Articles of Partnership and the Performance Trust Deed. Both have contractual legal standing to collect. At the point of a default the LP has absolutely no reason not to give over the title to the CI as required in the Articles of Partnership.

PROFESSIONAL REPORTS

Professional reports are used to analyze and approve the first property going into the LP. A Property Appraisal, Contractors Review Report, and the Preliminary Title Report are provided to the CI to help make the investment decision. The information is given to the CI so that the CI can make an informed decision as to whether to approve the property to be used as the CI collateral. The CI approval or rejection is based on three professional reports plus a visit to the property if desired. No CI approval means no commitment to invest. An amount of net equity greater than the CI funds and the amount of Bonus added together, would be a good guideline to financially qualify the property as collateral. The appraisal will help in this regard.

THERE IS NO LOAN INVOLVED IN THE LP

While the CI investment is like making a "loan" to the LP, it is not a loan. The CI funds are invested as a limited partner (CI is not making a loan to the LP) in return for a pre-agreed fixed Bonus payment. No loan is "assumed" or "taken subject to" or applied for by the LP in the EFT transaction for any reason. There is no requirement or need ever for the LP to take out a loan or become responsible for an existing loan when taking in and selling foreclosure property. The LP is not buying the property.

CONSIDERATION GIVEN BY THE OWNER IN THE LP AGREEMENT
The owner agrees to:
1. Use the property in foreclosure as collateral to secure the CI's funds.
   Favor the CI with financial and investment advantages.
2. Become an investor in the LP, using the sales proceeds of the property rescued from foreclosure, when the LP sells the property.
3. To allow investments to be made by the LP with the invested funds.
4. The owner agrees to take financial risk by investing in the LP.

CONSIDERATION RECEIVED BY THE OWNER IN THE LP AGREEMENT
The owner immediately receives relief because the following takes place as soon as the owner joins the LP:
1. The foreclosure is cured immediately, and the equity is rescued by the LP.
2. The property is put up of sale immediately per instructions in the LP Articles.
3. A Financial Support Plan to support loan payments ensures time to sell property.
4. A potential lawsuit for collection of a junior loan note is avoided.
5. Loan relief is achieved for the owner when the LP sells the property.
6. Time is granted to the owner to reestablish his/her financial position.
7. The use of an exclusive real estate plan is given to the owner free.
8. The owner earns profit from the LP.
9. All negative consequences of a foreclosure are resolved for the owner.
10. The owner has a way to join a financially sound group that immediately makes an insolvent owner into a qualified real estate investor.

CONSIDERATION GIVEN BY THE CI IN AGREEMENT
The CI agrees to:
1. Invest safely in the same LP with financially insolvent partners.

2. Approve the first property to be contributed to the LP.

3. Invest $60,000 in the LP to cure three property foreclosures, one at a time.

4. Provide the funds to the LP to pay curing the foreclosure.

5. Accept the property title as collateral, to replace the CI funds invested if the LP uses all the funds without achieving a property sale.

CONSIDERATION RECEIVED BY THE CI IN THE LP AGREEMENT

The CI receives;

1. An investment, the terms of which cannot be altered or changed by partners.

2. Right to choose and approve the collateral to be used as the CI security.

3. Sufficient (dual) collateral made up of property and cash that increase in amount as each property sale is completed by the LP.

4. Legal positions working in combination provide a high degree of safety.

5. A right to a pre-agreed amount of Bonus for providing investment funds.

6. The Bonus is paid from existing equities when 3 properties are sold by the LP.

7. Knowledge that each property taken into the LP will be offered for sale immediately.

8. A favored safety and financial position over all other LP partners.

9. An early return of capital and payment of a secured pre-agreed amount of Bonus.

10. An agreement that the CI fund be replenished after each LP sale.

11. A separate CI capital account with a separate accounting system for invested funds.

12. A Bonus acceleration opportunity at the completion of each LP.

WHAT THE LP/EFT DOES NOT DO

1. Equity sharing.

2. Foreclosure speculating for profit.

3. Short sales.

4. Flipping properties in any way.

5. Loan modification

NO ALTERNATIVE MOTIVE

1. The LP does not have a profit speculating plan designed to buy the owners' equity for pennies and then sell it, to turn the equity into a quick cash profit.

2. The property in foreclosure is not purchased (ever) by the LP or used to earn a fee or commission of any kind for the LP.

3. When the property is sold at full market value for the owner, the LP does not receive a dime of the net sales proceeds for itself.

4. In short, and making the point clear, the LP does not make or take any money at all in any way for any reason ever from the owner in foreclosure!

5. The truth is there is only one thing that will solve a foreclosure in favor of the property owner, money is the only thing that will solve the problem, and the LP "arranges" the money to cure the foreclosure and sell the property for full value for the owner's benefit.

INVESTMENT QUESTIONS ANSWERED

How can a property owner, who cannot cure a pending foreclosure to avoid all the nasty legal and financial consequences of a foreclosure, arrange it?

ANS: By Joining the LP/EFT as it has the only financial answer possible.

Where is a legally and financially safe and secure investment found that pays a fixed minimum reward of $25,500 to a maximum of $42,500 in about a year, with no personal management time or legal liability?

ANS: This question exactly describes what the CI receives in the LP.

How are extraordinarily large sums of investment capital accumulated on a repetitive never-ending basis for the first time to invest in real estate ventures be accomplished?

ANS: The LP/EFT can raise large amounts of investment capital in an LP Operating & Investment Fund on a regular occurring never-ending basis and is a unique first-time achievement.

The LP/EFT is very new and different and provides an important even vital answer to those who really need an honest answer to their horrible financial situation

PART FIVE
LEGAL SECTION

THE LIMITED PARTNERSHIP "LEGAL COMBINATION"
NOTICE: THE AUTHOR IS NOT A LAWYER

Therefore, each interested person in the LP/EFT should verify the legal statements put forward herein. There are sources to check the meaning of any of the legal terms used in the LP. Merriam- Webster's Dictionary of Law Definition is one, the Internet is another, and there most likely is a law library close to you. Or call an attorney to verify information given here.

AN LP ORIGINAL LEGAL POSITION

In the LP there is a "group of legal statues" used, that are not used in any other investment transaction of any kind. This grouping is a unique legal arrangement establishing a viable method to rescue 100% of the property equity from foreclosure for the owner. The grouping is original and is an exclusive way for the LP/EFT to perform the task of rescuing property equity from foreclosure. The Legal principals and laws used in the LP have never been used together in combination in a LP investment of any type before. This LP legal conglomeration also creates a new way for a CI to invest safely with a handsome timely reward! NOTE: The laws and principals are all statues and regulations in law. No made-up laws are in the LP.

In the LP, there is established a set of legal positions brought together for the first time ever. The LP uses current legal statutes and regulations to create a unique legal operating structure. This original legal combination is the key that opens the door to be able to create the financial and investment revelations that are achieved in the LP! The unique legal conglomeration establishes a different and better method to rescue property equity for the owner. The grouping also creates a safe way for a qualified CI to invest in a limited partnership safely!

UNFAMILIAR MATERIAL

Here are some legal terms used in the LP that are unusual to the real estate community. Some of these legal statues and regulations are never used by real estate brokers in normal everyday sale activity.

They are:
1) A Special Individual Purpose Set of Articles of Partnership (AP).
2) A Unique General Partner (GP) Power of Attorney in The AP.
3) A Special Use for A Performance Trust Deed (PTD).

4) A Special Use of The Bare Title Principal Of "Non-Possessory" Ownership.

5) A Grant Deed to Transfer a Fee Simple Ownership to A New Buyer.

6) A Condition Subsequent Agreement.

7) A Use of Fee Simple Executory Limitation, A Determinable Fee.

8) Two Separate Legal Contractual Standings in The Same Investment for The CI Are:

   a) The Article of Partnership

   b) A Performance Trust Deed

A LEGAL COMBINATION THAT WORKS

The LP "special legal structure" makes the ability to perform its task possible. Without the unique LP and its original set of:1) Articles of Partnership, 2) a Power Of Attorney that includes a special fiduciary relationship created, 3) a Bare Title Equitable Title division of ownership rights, 4) a Grant Deed with special required terms, use of Fee Simple Executory Limitation a Determinable Fee, 5) a securing of a pledge with a Performance Trust Deed, and a Condition Subsequent agreement to transfer and sell property, it would not be possible to complete this investment scenario.

This is the only original legal scenario that will work to avoid foreclosure and rescued the total property equity, solely for the property owner's benefit. Without the unique comprehensive legal arrangement, there would be no CI providing money and no way to perform the transaction. It is the Legal structure that creates the special LP and the CI position, and the money needed to perform the transaction.

LEGAL DIFFERENCE

In creating the LP/EFT an original legal scenario had to be designed, one that has never been constructed for the same purpose or use in the same way. The LP/EFT achieves the purpose of rescuing real property equity from foreclosure for the owner's exclusive benefit. However, the main purpose of the plan is to collect large sums of investment capital into an Operating and Investment Fund (O&IF) for a LP to invest and to share profits with the property owner limited partners.

The LP/EFT has original language, investment structure, legal construction, and operational techniques that are new and different. These individual parts together in a unique plan of operation create an exceptional first-time investment ability and result. The unique techniques created have never been duplicated in any other real estate investment.

The LP/EFT has a different legal configuration that affords both a currently financially insolvent property owner in foreclosure and a qualified CI a unique way to safely invest together. Rescuing property equity from being foreclosed and turning it into investment capital is what the LP/EFT does. The LP also raises large sums of capital to invest this way. The investment capital gathered is invested for the benefit of the owners rescued from foreclosure.

This is the one and only original legal scenario that will work to avoid foreclosure and rescued the total property equity (100%) for the property owner's benefit. The LP "special legal arrangement" makes it possible; it cannot be done without this legal combination.

The combination:

- A has an original set of Articles of Partnership,
- A Power of Attorney that includes a special fiduciary relationship created,
- A Bare Title division of ownership rights,
- A Grant Deed with special required terms,
- A use of Fee Simple Executory Limitation, a Determinable Fee,
- A securing of a pledge with a Performance Trust Deed,
- A Condition Subsequent agreement for the LP to sell property.

Without the unique comprehensive legal arrangement there would be no new type of secured CI providing investment money to start the LP. And no way for the LP to arrange a financial answer for the LP to use to cure a foreclosure and rescue the owner's property equity. It is the "legal combination of legal statutes" that creates ability to perform the transaction. The legal scenario is the key ingredient! And no other such legal grouping for the purpose of saving property equity has ever been established before. Also, without this legal structure it would not be possible to gather large sums of "Operating and Investment Capital" on an ongoing never-ending repetitive basis for the LP to invest in profit ventures of all types. This much capital over a period really opens a whole new world of investment inside and outside of the LP for many different purposes.

MAJOR ORIGINAL LEGAL ACCOMPLISHMENTS

The following legal advantages cannot be accomplished in any other Limited Partnership, or real estate transaction of any kind, without the legal grouping described herein. **Both limited partner needs, intentions, and desires can be accomplished by:**

- Legally establishing a new type of collateral concept by creating a "Priority Use Position" for one partner in a LP.
- Legally establishing two ways to be successful in a Limited Partnership for a CI. The CI gets the reward or collection of the collateral, one or the other!
- Establishing a legal right to "property title fee ownership", not just an "equity lien position", to protect the CI capital invested.
- Creating a new reward system and paying one partner first with a pre-agreed amount of reward while other partners share profits.

- Changing a financially non-qualified insolvent (property owner in foreclosure) into a legally qualified investor in an LP.
- Arranging a new fast and easier legal method to collect the CI collateral by creating two legal standings in an LP.
- The LP has an original legal structure designed to achieve the purpose of rescuing equities from foreclosure and investing the equities for the property owner. (This one has never been done before and is a new legal structure inside a LP)
- Creates two legal classes of limited partners with different money contributions and legal positions in the Partnership. (This one has never been done before in this way and is a new legal structure inside a LP)
- Combines two different legal standings in the same investment. The Articles of Partnership and the Performance Trust Deed each offers a different legal standing to protect the CI. (This one has never been done before and is a new legal structure inside a LP)
- Creates a new legal method to secure a single limited partner CI inside a LP while not securing the other limited partners. (This one has never been done before and is a new legal structure inside a LP).
- Created a new legal reward system to pay two different classes of limited partners in two different ways in the same partnership. (This one has never been done before and is a new legal structure inside a LP)
- Created a new sequence of legal events that feature new uses for several legal definitions of law that when combined create a new way of curing a foreclosure and rescuing property equity from loss, for the sole benefit of the property owners. (This one has never been done before and is a new legal structure inside a LP)
- Created a new legal way for a CI to invest in Trust Deeds without being concerned about being involved in a legal, costly, and time-consuming foreclosure or bankruptcy action to collect the collateral behind the Trust
- Deed. (This one has never been done before and is a new legal structure inside a LP)

HIGHLIGHTING EXCLUSIVE LEGAL ADVANTAGES.

These legal advantages cannot be accomplished in any other LP, without the legal grouping described herein. The LP offers a safe and legal way of advancing funds to cure a foreclosure for the owner, when no lender would lend more money to the owner, so the owner could pay the current loan arrearages.

The LP creates and provides the following new and exciting advantages that were never possible.

- Having a Limited Partnership act as a legal force in an original way representing both classes of partners to accomplish their personal needs and intentions.
- Using a Performance Deed of Trust in a new way, to be able to bring limited partners with different roles together in a LP, and to accomplish the needs, intentions, and desires of both type of partners.
- Legally establishing a new type of collateral concept by creating a "Priority Use Position" for one partner in a LP.
- Legally establishing a second way to be successful for an CI in a LP. The CI gets the reward or the collateral one or the other!
- Establishing a legal right to a property title of ownership as collateral for the CI investing capital in the LP.
- Creating a new reward system and paying one partner first with a pre-agreed fixed amount of reward while other limited partners must wait to share LP profits.
- Changing a financially non-qualified currently financially insolvent investor (property owner in foreclosure) into a legally qualified investor in a LP.
- Arranging a new legal method of collection of the reward promised by creating two legal standings for a secured CI in a LP.

EXCLUSIVE LEGAL "STEP BY STEP" PROCESS

Steps of taking a property Bare Title and then transferring a Fee Simple Ownership by Grant Deed to a new buyer. The following legal statutes are used to form a group that gives the legal ability it needs to achieve its purpose.

Step 1 First Legal Item: The Articles of Partnership (AP) ©.

This is necessary to spell out how the LP operates and what the legal terms and conditions of the participants are in the LP.

Step 2 Second Legal Item: Power of Attorney.

A legal standing is necessary to spell out who is in charge and who is responsible for the LP performance.

Step 3 Third Legal Item: Grant Deed.

This is a legal document necessary to transfer the title of ownership to the party named in the Articles of Partnership.

Step 4 Fourth Legal Item: Bare Title

The Bare Title is necessary to spell out a particular type of ownership that is being transferred.

Step 5 Fifth Legal Item: Performance Trust Deed.

This is necessary to secure the investor's investment by recording a PTD against the property acting as collateral.

Step 6 Sixth Legal Item: Fee Simple Executory Limitation

This is necessary because a Fee Simple Executory Limitation position is established in the AP to complete a Condition Subsequent created in the AP that mandates a sale of the property for the owners by the LP.

Step 7 Seventh Legal Item: Condition subsequence

Condition subsequence refers to an event or situation that brings an end to something else. A condition subsequent is often used in a legal context as a marker bringing an end to one's legal rights or duties.

Step 8 Eighth Legal Item: Real Estate Sales Contract.

Need a regular sale contract to make the property transfer of sale.

DETAILED LEGAL EXPLANATIONS

Here are the steps of taking a property Bare Title and then transferring a Fee Simple Ownership by Grant Deed to a new buyer. The following legal statutes gives the LP legal ability it needs to achieve receiving and transferring the LP Bare Title.

Step 1 First Legal Item: The Articles of Partnership © (AP).

The partners involved enter a legal contract, the AP. The CI, the property owner whose property is in foreclosure, and the General Partner of the LP all sign the AP articles. The AP sets out the purpose of each limited partner and is designed structurally in a unique way that creates an innovative legal position to achieve each limited partner's purpose. The AP creates a strong legal position so each limited partner can achieve their intended purpose. The AP dictates that the owner transfers the property's Bare Title to the LP to cure the foreclosure and hold the Bare Title until it is sold by the LP

The AP is drawn in such a way as to legally and financially allow this to happen. The AP describes and protects each partner's legal, financial, and investment position. The acknowledgment is accomplished at the escrow company's office.

The AP is the legal agreement between all the partners used to accomplish the purpose that they have all agreed on. It is a contract between a General Partner and persons who place their investment capital into the LP.

The understanding is that there will be a sharing of the profits between the limited property owners and the LP. The CI is to receive a pre-agreed fixed amount Bonus for investing cash to cure the property, at a critical moment in time, to sell it for full value for the benefit of the owners. A specially designed and newly constructed LP grants special advantages for just one class of limited partner, the CI. There are two classes of limited partners in the LP, the property owner taken out of foreclosure being the other class.

A unique legal, financial, and investment construction in the LP provides:

1) A full value sale for the owner to rescue all the property equity from foreclosure for the sole benefit of the owner.

2) A new secured CI position in the LP makes investing in foreclosures safer and more rewarding than standard real estate investing.

3) A new ever-growing never-ending Operating & Investment Fund (O&IF) is created by rescuing equities and the owner investing the equity in the LP, for the owner's benefit.

Step 2 Second Legal Item: Power of Attorney (AP).

A Power of Attorney establishes a legal authority. The Power of Attorney granted to the LP General Partner in the Articles gives the power and responsibility to complete all the terms and conditions set down in the AP to the GP. The GP must adhere to the terms and conditions laid down in the AP. It directs the property in foreclosure to be taken out of foreclosure and sold by the LP.

Step 3 Third Legal Item: Grant Deed.

The LP first receives a Grant Deed transferring only the Bare Title to the property subject to terms and conditions in the AP. The property owner transfers the Bare Title to the LP to hold the title as a fiduciary for sale and disposition. The escrow records the transfer of the Grant Deed signed by the owner to the LP, as required in the escrow instructions and in the AP.

Explanation of deed: Blackstone defines a deed as a "writing or instrument under seal, containing some contract of agreement, and which the parties have delivered." Thus, the word "deed", in a legal sense, may mean any sealed contract or instrument, such as a lease, mortgage, or bond. The popular sense restricts it to a conveyance of property. A Grant Deed subject to terms and conditions that established what the grantor/grantee ownership is between them. A conveyance is a right, title, or interest in real or personal property from one person or entity to another. A deed may then be defined as writing by which lands, tenements, and hereditaments are conveyed, which writing is signed, sealed, and delivered by the parties. The ordinary common deed contains several clauses that have an important bearing on the rights of the parties.

Step 4 Fourth Legal Item: Bare Title. Bare Title Understanding:

A title can be passed from the Grantor to the Grantee without passing the full bundle of legal rights. The bundle of legal rights consists of all the equitable ownership rights and the legal title to the property. No ownership equitable interest needs to pass if that is what is agreed to between the Grantor and Grantee. The Grantor can transfer only the Bare Legal Title to the Grantee.

Definition:

Bare Title is a type of non-possessory ownership. Bare title lacks the usual rights and privileges of ownership. A trustee or fiduciary in a deed of trust securing instrument may hold the title to a secured property but only such title as is needed to carry to the terms of the lien document (contract). The AP conditions the Grant Deed transfer to the LP with a Bare Title "Non-Possessory" position meaning the LP holds the property title only to sell and transfer the title on behalf of the owner to a new buyer. POSSESSION: The act or state of <u>owning or holding</u> something. The LP will become the "holder on condition for disposition" for the property owner when it receives the Grant Deed from escrow.

The legal structure arranged in the EFT is a new exceptional and original grouping of legal statues and regulations. The CI is given a special legal position that afford maximum protection in the LP. The CI has two legal standings in the investment. The Articles of Partnership is a legal binding contact with terms and conditions that favor the CI's. Also, the CI receives a Performance Trust Deed that is a legal standing outside of the LP. These two legal standings give control of collateral collection in case of a LP default. These two together for first time-ever, separate CI legal contractual standings and solidify the investment legal standing for the CI.

In property law, a title is a bundle of rights in a piece of property in which a person or entity may own either a legal interest or equitable interest. The rights in the bundle may be separated and held by different parties. Title may also refer to a formal document, such as a deed, that serves as evidence of ownership. Conveyance of the document may be required to transfer ownership in the property to another person. Title is distinct from possession, a right that often accompanies ownership but is not necessarily sufficient to prove it. In many cases, both possession and title may be transferred independently of each other. For real property, land registration and recording provide public notice of ownership information.

Ownership of property may be private, collective, or common, and the property may be of objects, land or real estate, or intellectual property. Determining ownership in law involves determining who has certain rights and duties over the property. These rights and duties, sometimes called a "bundle of rights", can be separated and held by different parties.

The LP Articles of Partnership conditions the Grant Deed transfer from the owner to the LP with a Bare Title, a holding title position. The LP has no equitable ownership interest and by agreement is only holding the legal title for disposition.

Merriam-Webster Dictionary of Law Definition of TITLE: The means or right by which one owns or possesses property, broadly: the quality of ownership as determined by a body of facts and events. Bare title to the property lacks the usual rights and privileges of ownership. A trustee in a deed of trust securing instrument may hold the title to a secured property, but only such title as is needed to carry out the terms of the lien document.

The owner's purpose in transferring Bare Title to the LP is to have the "property fee ownership" pledged as collateral, after the is foreclosure is cured, to attract investment capital into the LP. Upon the Grant Deed Bare Title transfer to the LP the owner is fulfilling a condition laid down in the AP.

Equitable Title is title vested in one who is considered by the application of equitable principles to be the owner of property even though legal title is vested in another. You have the legal title if your name appears as the grantee on a deed. The legal title is "apparent" ownership or ownership that is documented on paper. You may assume that your ownership of a property is complete with legal title, but this is not the case. Another party may have equitable title restricting some of the ways you can use and enjoy the property.

The main difference between an equitable vs. a legal title is that the latter is the only one that gives actual ownership of the property. There are many smaller, more intricate differences that can vary on a case-by- case basis. In general, the equitable title gives a person the right to use the land and enjoy the benefits that come along with its ownership. The legal title does not necessarily grant these rights. An equitable title does not allow the titleholder to sell or transfer ownership. Legal title is the only title that can do this. The LP sells the property for the owner's benefit! Legal title has the advantage over equitable in that it allows the legal titleholder to demand compensation from parties that purchase or lease the property.

Equitable ownership is not "true ownership." In other words, someone with the equitable title could not argue that he or she was the legal owner or possessor of the property in a court of law. True ownership requires a legal title. The equitable title does, however, grant the person more consistent control over the property. That's right, equitable title can be more important than the legal title.

Step 5 Fifth Legal Item: Performance Trust Deed.

A Performance Trust Deed or mortgage is security for the "performance of an act or obligation and therefore it may secure a money debt or any other obligation. Generally, it secures the obligations of a promissory note, but it also can secure other obligations of the trustor such as a lease, the performance of a contract, or future obligations created by contract, or it can be used to indemnify the beneficiary against possible contingencies.

The LP gives into escrow a PTD in favor of the CI and it is recorded against the property in the land recorder's office. A PTD secures a pledge of collateral (the property fee ownership) made to the CI by the LP in the AP. They LP could not secure the collateral pledged, the property fee simple ownership, without first taking the Bare Title to transfer the ownership to a new buyer. There is a reference in the PTD identifying the necessary Articles in the AP that gives the legal right and responsibility to the GP to take the title and sell the property. The PTD secures the start-up funds provided by the CI with the pledge of collateral to the CI. The escrow records the transfer of the PTD as instructed to do in the escrow instructions.

Step 6 Sixth Legal Item: Fee Simple Executory Limitation:

A defeasible fee created with clear durational language expressing a condition (e.g. "so long as", "until", "while"), which causes ownership of a property to vest in a third party identified by the grantor if that condition comes about. A Fee Simple Executory Limitation position is established in the AP to complete a Condition Subsequent created in the AP that mandates a sale of the property for the owners by the LP.

In the transaction when the Condition Subsequent, specifically the sale of the property, the automatic right to transfer the property's absolute fee simple title becomes possible. This right is established in the AP and the Fee Simple Executory Limitation position.

Merriam-Webster's Dictionary of Law Definition of Determinable Fee: A defeasible fee that terminates automatically upon the occurrence of a specified event. Three types of defeasible estates are the 1) fee simple determinable, 2) fee simple subject to an executory limitation or interest, and 3) fee simple subject to a condition subsequent.

Defeasible Fee: An estate in land that may be divested from its current owner upon the occurrence of an event set forth by the grantor in the grantee. An estate in land that may be divested from its current owner upon the occurrence of an event set forth by the grantor in the grant. A Fee Simple Executory Limitation position is established in the LP Articles of Partnership to complete a Condition Subsequent created in the AP that mandates for the LP to take Bare Title and to sell the property for the owner's benefit.

A defeasible estate is created when a grantor transfers land conditionally. Upon the happening of the event or condition stated by the grantor. Because a defeasible estate always grants less than a full fee simple, a defeasible estate will always create one or more future interests.

A fee simple determinable is an estate that will end automatically when the stated event or condition occurs. A fee simple subject to an executory limitation is an estate that ends when a specific condition is met and then transfers to a third party. The interest will not revert to the grantor. If the condition is met, the grantee loses interest, and the third party gains it automatically.

Merriam-Webster Dictionary of Law Definition of Fee Simple: Simple without limitation (as to heirs) and **Unrestricted (as to transfer of ownership):** a fee that is alienable (as by deed, will, or intestacy) and of potentially indefinite duration.

Merriam-Webster Dictionary of Law Definition of Executory Limitation: A limitation that creates an executory interest. (A fee simple subject to an executory limitation).

Step 7 Seventh Legal Item: Condition subsequence

Condition subsequence refers to an event or situation that brings an end to something else. A condition subsequent is often used in a legal context as a marker bringing an end to one's legal rights or duties. A condition subsequent may be either an event or a situation that must either (1) occur or (2) fail to continue to occur. When the Condition Subsequent, specifically the sale of the property, is completed the automatic right to transfer the property's fee simple title is established in the LP Article of Partnership and law.

In the Articles of Partnership, there is set up a Condition Subsequence that instructs the LP General Partner to arrange for the sale of the property for the owner. And when the sale occurs to deliver the fee simple ownership of the property by Grant Deed to a new owner. When the Condition Subsequent, specifically the sale of the property by the LP, is completed the automatic right to transfer the property's absolute fee simple title that is established in law and in the Articles of Partnership.

Step 8 Eighth Legal Item: Real Estate Sales Contract.

The LP lists and sells, through a real estate broker, the owner's property and transfers by Grant Deed Fee Simple Ownership of the property to the new owner.

It has been shown here that without the "legal combination" arranged and developed in the LP, the rescue of 100% of property equity from a foreclosure cannot happen. The new way to invest safely in a pending foreclosure property and the new way to grow the operating and investment capital fund also would not be possible.

PART 6
GENERAL COMMENTS SECTION

The value of this transaction although primarily it deals with rescuing foreclosure property equities is in the ability to raise capital to invest. These limited partnership investment funds are used to participate in solving many different types of properties that need financial help.

FIRST-TIME EVER

Never has there been a way to tie together and invest thousands of property equities throughout the United States, about to be lost through foreclosure, into investment capital. This phenomenon has opened a new way to do business in real estate and as well has created many original individual real estate transactions to introduce to the market. This happens when there is created an ever-growing capital fund to invest because of helping others.

FROM AN INVESTOR POINT OF VIEW

If one would look at the position of the General Partner company "Foreclosure Answer Affirmed, Inc.", one would see that when several Limited Partnerships will be ongoing and complimenting one an another in several important ways from an investment point of view.

Which limited partnership would let an investor end up with owning a property because of a default. It will not happen! This makes it very attractive from an investor point of view. It is a guarantee like investment.

THE PROPERTY OWNERS' DECISION

Anyone interested in a new development in the marketplace will first want to analyze the financial aspects of the new development. In the case of the Extraordinary Investment Transaction the following information is offered so that a fair and just conclusion of the validity of the transaction can be made without any apprehension.

In the Extraordinary Investment Transaction, the property owner facing a Notice Of Default on his/her property, without any means to curing the Notice Of Default, has a very difficult financial decision. Should I join a partnership and become an investor using my property as a capital Investment or stand firm and possibly lose all the equity by forfeiting the property to a foreclosure. Or should I except a few dollars and sell to avoid a foreclosure on my record. The only two choices an owner has are financially very bad.

I submit that most people with a substantial amount of equity, and no way of curing the Notice Of Default, would choose to save the equity and improve their financial future by taking advantage of the opportunity to rescue and reinvest in real estate. The average value of a residential property in the United Stated is $420,000. The amount of equity today ranges from $100,000 or more in a great many pending foreclosures. There are several hundreds of thousands of Notices of Defaults started every year in the United States.

One of the reasons the owner has for joining the Extraordinary Investment Transaction would be because the equity money lost by foreclosure would take a very long time to replace. Saving up the lost amount of equity would take many years. Also, the nasty financial and legal aftereffects of foreclosure are hideous and are solved by and in the Extraordinary Investment Transaction for the owners.

Makes no sense to say no to joining the LP that features the Extraordinary Investment Transaction that can save 100% of the property equity and that allows time for restructuring a personal financial standing. I believe that 10 out 10 of qualifying property owners with thousands of dollars to lose will choose to help themselves by joining the LP/EIT.

ANALYZING THE EXTRAORDINARY INVESTMENT TRANSACTION FROM A FINANCIAL POINT OF VIEW.

STEP 1
The PCI invests $60,000 in a LP.

The property is taken out of foreclosure and will sell for the appraised price of $420,000.

The property is sold for $420,000 and $100,000 (100%) is the rescued equity amount. The full value of the property according to appraisal is $420,000 and is the amount invested in the LP by the owner by contributing the title to the property to the LP.

It takes say $29,400 to pay the selling costs. The $70,600 is the adjustment equity amount rescued after subtracting the $29,400 amount from $100,000 rescued to pay the Notice Of Default amount and costs of sale.

The $70,600 rescued is 100% of the equity in a normal sale!!!! No one is taken a dime of the owner equity! The $70,600 rescued becomes invested capital from the property owner in the LP.

STEP 2 Rescue Process
Same as Step 1
Now $70,600 times 2 LP properties sold equals $141,200 in the LP operating and investment fund.

STEP 3 Rescue Process

Same as Step 1

Now $70,600 times 3 property sales total $211,800 in LP. The 3 property sales made by the LP equals $211,800 in owner investment funds and becomes the investment operating & investment fund in the LP!

Here Are The LP Numbers For One LP With 30 Owners/Properties Sold

30 properties in the LP X $70,600 property equities rescued equals 2,118,000. This is the money that is raised and invested in the LP by the owners. The O&IF is invested to earn profit for the owners. 10 LP's fully funded is 10 X $2,118,000 equals $21,180,000 in Operating And Investment Capital.

No where in this transaction is there a promise to one investor a high interest rate, and to a second investor a higher rate than the first rate to raise more capital. An illegal scheme. The LP pays a fixed rate 42.5% percentage bonus of $25,500 to only one investor position in each LP.

BONUS PAYMENT

The $25,500 is paid out of the $211,800 from the three sales made by the LP. The PCI is paid $25,500 out of the 3rd property sale at the time of the third sale. This is the owner's money, and it is used to initially pay the PCI Bonus. It is an expense of the owner because the owner is the benefactor of the PCI's help.

However, the LP will pay the $25,500 out of gross profits of the partnership to the owners. The LP will credit back to the owner's capital account the money ($25,500) used from the owner's property sale money. The LP itself also enjoys a financial benefit from the Partnership Extraordinary Investment Transaction.

As already stated, when the partnership earns gross profits from investing for profit it refunds the $25,500 to the owner's capital account, in effect paying back the PCI bonus money taken from owner property sales.

The LP reimbursement of the $25,500 will come from gross profit of the LP earned though investments. There is no cost to the property owners to pay the PCI $25,500. Or a proper way to look at it is that it is an expense of the partnership, and no person is paying the PCI. There is no place in the transaction where a single property owner pays anything except normal sale closing costs.

The PCI earns the bonus, and it is paid from LP investment profits. The owner gets $100,000 rescued and saves paying $25,500 to the PCI for the Bonus the PCI earned helping the owner.

POINTS

- This is an owner who turned investor using his/her property as an investment rather than loss of all the remaining equity to a foreclosure or profit speculator for next to nothing.

- There is no place in the transaction where a single owner pays the PCI $25,500.

- The owners take the financial risk of how the LP performs. If the LP loses the owners lose. The PCI is safe if there is a LP default.

- Most people upon reviewing the PCI financial and legal positions would conclude that the PCI has a low risk for a high reward!

FINAL ANALYSIS EXAMPLE

The figures here are estimates made-up from what might be an approximate result of an average property situation. One might think this number is a little low or that number is a little high but really an awful lot of money is rescued for an awful lot of people and a lot of great investments are made that normally would not be made because there was no way to do it! Now there is a way! This Extraordinary Investment Transaction does an awful lot for an awful lot of people.

HOW COME

How come this transaction has not been accomplished before. Who knows? I suggest it is because of the legal combination design that allows the transaction to work. It was not easy to figure out what legal statues were necessary and how the various legal statues would work together. This stalled a lot of thinking about how to find a way to achieve the Extraordinary Investment Transaction.

NEW TRANSACTIONAL ABILITIES

SPIN-OFF INVESTMENT PLANS
1031 EXCHANGE PLAN

This plan will allow an exchange broker to use high value "cash out" properties to create an exchange. High value cash out properties are hard to find because hardly anyone wants to pay the capital gain tax. The LP will be selling high value properties to rescue the equities, and the real estate exchange broker can use these properties.

Having a source for the cash out property waiting will allow the exchanger to build up from a lower priced property to the high value cash out property. The cash out property will be waiting for the exchanger to build to and close as soon as the cash out property is needed. The necessary exchange properties needed to exchange up to the "cash out" property can be located with confidence that there is the cash out property waiting.

PORTFOLIO PROPERTY ADJUSTMENT PLAN

Solves negative cash flow problem dragging down the positive cash flow. Many investors have four or five properties in their investment portfolio. The LP can take in the properties that have negative cash flow and leave the investor with only the cash flowing properties. This will help the owner's financial and credit standing.

DOLLAR FOR DOLLAR PLUS FINANCING JOINT VENTURING PLAN

Any Investor who joint ventures with the LP is safer because the LP will take the majority part of the risk by providing a financial source of funds needed for the completion of the investment.

IN NOT THE SAME
What The /EFT Does Not Do!

Equity Sharing.

Foreclosure Speculating for profit.

Short Sales.

Flipping Property in any way.

Or any other investment transaction.

APPENDIX
FINANCIAL STRUCTURAL CHARTS

THE PERFORMANCE TRUST DEED©

Property 1 - CI Receives Performance Trust Deed
In the first property sale escrow, the PCI re-conveys the PTD to the EGLP.

Property 2 - CI Receives Performance Trust Deed
In **more than one property at a time has a PTD**
the second property sale escrow, the PCI re-conveys the PTD to the EGLP.

Property 3 - CI Receives Performance Trust Deed
After the first sale is made the LP can take in two properties at a time. The CI will receive a PTD on both properties. After the second sale the LP will even be able to take in more properties looking to sell the third property. For each property taken into the LP the CI will receive a PTD until three properties sell. So, when the third property is sold, the PCI will have re-conveyed all PTD'S held.

THE EQUITY GROWTH LIMITED PARTNERSHIP©
PCI COLLATERAL ACCELERATES AND LOWERS RISK

Property 1 - $60,000 CI Funds invested in the EGLP
Property Gross Equity of $100,000 in property 1
Total = Cash & Equity of $160,000 secures CI $60,000

Property 2 - $60,000 is replenished from Property 1 sale
+ Property Gross Equity of $100,000 in Property 2
+ $70,000 Sale funds netted from Property 1 sale
Total = Cash and Equity of $230,000 secures CI $60,000

Property 3 - $60,000 replenished from Property 2 sale
+ Property Gross Equity of $100,000 in Property 3
+ $70,000 Sale funds netted from Property 1
+ $65,000 Sale funds netted from Property 2
Total = Cash and Equity of $295,000 secures CI $60,000

As you can see from this chart each time an LP sells a property the risk factor goes down for the CI. Every investment has risk, no matter how small the risk! However, this formula creates an extremely low risk for the CI that would be hard to duplicate in other investments.

THE CASH INVESTOR INVESTMENT FUND
THE CI $60,000 INVESTED IS REPLENISHED AFTER EACH PROPERTY SALE

STEP 1: PROPERTY FINANCIAL STATUS
L1) $321,000 APPRAISED VALUE
L2) $ 9,600 Minus Loan Arrearage (CI FUND USED)
L3) $215,070 Minus All Loan Amounts
L4) $ 96,330 ESTIMATE OF "GROSS" EQUITY

STEP 2: ESTIMATE OF QWNER'S "NET EQUITY"
L5) $ 96,330 AVAILABLE GROSS EQUITY **(L4)**
L6) $ 22,470 minus 7% broker commission
L7) $ 3,000 minus sales preparation (CCC USED)
L8) $ 4,000 minus title transfer cost to EGLP (CCC USED)
L9) $ 66,860 BALANCE IS NET EQUITY AFTER SALE

STEP 3: ACTUAL SALE OF THE PROPERTY TO A NEW BUYER
L10) $105,930 SALE GROSS EQUITY **(L2 plus L4)**
L11) $ 4,000 minus sales closing costs (directly from sale proceeds)
L12) $ 22470 minus 7% commission
L13) $ 16,600 minus CI fund replenishment **(L2 plus L7 plus L8)**
L14) $ 62,860 NET EQUITY AFTER SALE

STEP 4: MONEY USED FROM THE CI FUND IS REPLENISHED
$60,000 CI investment fund
$ 9,600 minus loan arrears **(L2)**
$ 3,000 minus sales preparation **(L7)**
$ 4,000 minus title transfer cost to the LP **(L8)**
$43,400 The balance after expenses paid out of the CI fund
$16,600 CI fund is replenished out of the property sale proceeds
$60,000 ORIGINAL CI FUND STARTING AMOUNT

CAPITAL ACCOUNT FOR PROPERTY OWNER AFTER SALE
$105,930 Gross equity to start

$ 43,070 Total selling expense **(L11 + L12 + L13)**

$ 62,860 Net equity equals owners' investment in the LP

THE LIMITED PARTNERSHIP
CI BONUS ACCELERATION CHART

	Amount Invested	Bonus	Total Bonus Earned	Timing to Complete Each LP
1st LP Completed	$60,000	$25,500	$25,500	Approximately Three Months
2nd LP Completed	$85,500	$36,337	$61,837	Approximately Nine Months
3rd LP Completed	$121,337	$51,568	$113,405	Approximately One Year

CI EARNS $453,605 IN APPROXIMATELY THREE YEARS
AS A CI JUST STANDS BY AND WATCHS THE LP'S WORK!

$ 60,000 Original CI start amount to do the first LP

$113,405 First LP earning amount

_____

$173,405 Now 3 LPs cab be started at once (Each One Financially Is Safer And Safer)

$340,205 3 LP earnings

$113,405 Original first LP earnings

_____

$453,605 TOTAL 4 LP'S COMPLETED

In LP'S The Performance Time, Numbers Grow And Accelerate!
 - ◆ The Bonus amount accelerates!
 - ◆ The cash on hand in the LP accelerates!
 - ◆ The number of properties taken into the LP accelerates!
 - ◆ The number of LP opened accelerates!
 - ◆ The Operating and Investment Fund (O&IF) accelerates!
 - ◆ The number of LP investments accelerates!
 - ◆ The number CI Performance Trust Deeds accelerates

The performance time and numbers accelerate in each LP started!

Robert L. Evans

r.leeevans@aol.com

OWNER ADVANCEMENT
THE OWNER'S FORECLOSURE PROBLEM IS SOLVED

➝ *Now the owner has a real choice of selling for full value and investing the rescued money by choosing this foreclosure transaction.*
➝ *The foreclosure is cured, and a full value sale is accomplished.*
➝ *Owner rescues 100% of the property equity to invest.*
➝ *A new investment position earns a profit share.*
➝ *All the negative legal and financial consequence are eliminated*

INVESTMENT ADVANCEMENT
THE SECURED INVESTOR BENEFITS ARE ATTRACTIVE!

➝ *Original structures create legal, financial, investment safety.*
➝ *Investor "bonus reward is fixed" up to $42,500.*
➝ *Investor timing to collect is approximately one year.*
➝ *Investor has a "property fee title of ownership" as collateral.*
➝ *No investor bankruptcy or foreclosure involvement is possible.*
➝ *Normal investment pitfalls are eliminated.*

TRANSACTION ADVANCEMENT
EARN BY HELPING OTHERS SUCCEED

➝ *Investing has never been better than this. The risk is low, the return is substantial, the legal position is strong, and the timing is very good. This transaction checks all the boxes for the investor.*

Finally,
An Honest Financial Answer For The Owner, Investor, Lender, and Real Estate Broker. Everyone wins!

R. Lee Evans